Sue Palmer
Pie Corbett

Literacy: what works?

About the Authors

Sue Palmer was a primary teacher and head teacher in Scotland until 1984, when she returned to her home town of Manchester to do an MEd in Reading and Linguistics. She then moved to Cornwall, married another primary teacher, had a baby, and spent the next ten years scraping a living at home by teaching dyslexic children and writing and editing teaching materials. In 1990, she ran a national campaign for *Balance in the teaching of language and literacy skills*.

In 1995, Sue began touring the country with her *Language Live Roadshows* on spelling (for Y3 and Y4) and punctuation (for Y5 and Y6). Although hugely enjoyable, three years of this practically killed her and she was glad when the advent of the National Literacy Strategy provided a quieter way of earning a living: courses for teachers on grammar, spelling and phonics, and articles in the educational press.

Sue has since written many more books and educational TV programmes on aspects of literacy, and contributed to several NLS training packages. She still writes regularly in the *Times Educational Supplement*, provides courses in schools, universities and LEAs throughout the UK and acts as a literacy consultant to educational publishers and the BBC. Sue's most recent publications include *Big Book Spelling* (Ginn), the *Connections* series for cross-curricular literacy (OUP), the *Skeleton Poster Books* and OHTs for text-types and grammar (TTS), and two books for David Fulton on cross-curricular writing.

Pie Corbett was a primary school teacher, working with the poet Brian Moses. The children he taught won awards annually in the WHSmith Young Writers competition in all the schools that he served – as well winning the Poetry Society competition, Cadbury awards and being televised. He gained a reputation for the sort of creative teaching described in *Catapults and Kingfishers* (OUP) and *Poetic Writing in the Primary School* (KRLDC). He was a head teacher in Kent before working as a Staff Development Co-ordinator in East Kent. He moved to the Cotswolds to work as senior lecturer at The Cheltenham and Gloucester College of Higher Education. Here he co-ordinated the  Primary English team, led the Articled Teacher PGCE and the two-year school-based BEd programmes. After a secondment to Ofsted, he became English Inspector in Gloucestershire.

Pie has written many books, schemes and articles about literacy, and made several programmes for the BBC, with different writers. He contributed to various aspects of the NLS, writing materials, producing videos and running training for literacy consultants. He co-ordinates projects, such as the 'Storymaking Project' (I.R.L.C.), investigating learning English and other languages.

Pie's most recent publications include *Searchlights for Spelling* (Cambridge), the *Grammar Success* series (OUP) and two books on teaching story writing (David Fulton). As a poet, his most recent anthology is *The Works 2* (Macmillan), while *Poems for Year 4* (Macmillan) was shortlisted for the annual CLPE award for excellence in poetry. *The King's Pyjamas* and *How to Write Thrillers* were both chosen as books of the year by *Junior Education*. He runs training, and works as a poet and storyteller in schools.

Contents

About the authors   2

Foreword   4

Chapter 1: The National Literacy Strategy   5

Chapter 2: Phonics, Handwriting and Spelling   15

Chapter 3: Grammar for Literacy   27

Chapter 4: Cross-curricular Literacy   37

Chapter 5: Creativity and Literacy   47

Chapter 6: Speaking, Listening and Literacy   57

Chapter 7: Planning, Assessment, Marking and SATs   69

Chapter 8: Post Script   79

Appendix 1: Drama Activities   88

Appendix 2: Talking Sentences and Stories   89

Appendix 3: Promoting Reading   90

Appendix 4: National Literacy Strategy Publications   92

Appendix 5: Recommended Resources   95

Foreword

This book was written to accompany a series of conferences – *Literacy: what have we learned and where do we go next?* – in autumn 2003. In Chapters 1 to 7 the left-hand pages mirror some of the OHTs used in the conferences, and the right-hand pages provide a commentary. The final session of the conferences was interactive: some areas we suspected it might cover are touched on in Chapter 8.

The book reflects our experiences as independent literacy specialists during the years 1998 to 2003, when we were travelling around the UK speaking to and working with thousands of teachers. During the same period, we also contributed as independent consultants to the National Literacy Strategy, working closely with Literacy Consultants and the NLS Directors. We thus had the chance to see the Strategy from both sides.

It is not an academic book, so we have not included academic references to the research which often underpins our thinking. However, anyone requiring a specific reference can contact us by email at the addresses below and we'll do our best to provide further information.

The opinions expressed here are our own, very much influenced by our own teaching practices, by our experiences of the Literacy Strategy and by the teachers we have met. Where we have been critical, it is not intended to downplay the importance of the Strategy in trying to raise standards in literacy. We have taken part in that challenge, and feel that it has been better to try than to snipe from the sidelines. Our thinking is therefore offered to stimulate debate about the pedagogy and practice of literacy teaching and how we might all best take the next steps forwards.

Sue Palmer and Pie Corbett, June 2003

sue@suepalmer.co.uk
pikeorbit@tinyworld.co.uk

The National Literacy Strategy

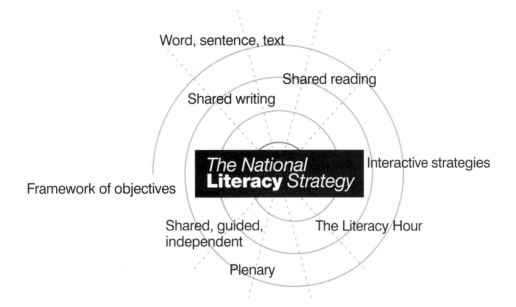

The National Literacy Strategy, introduced in English schools in September 1998, has had a profound influence on teaching practice throughout the country. Five years on, this book attempts to summarise what teachers have found useful in improving their literacy teaching, and to look forward to ways in which the profession might make further improvements. This first chapter covers some practical aspects of the Strategy which have affected every school; subsequent chapters look more closely at specific areas of literacy teaching.

As we have worked on the book, we've been amazed at how much territory the teaching profession has covered in this short period. Literacy teaching, in all its aspects, has been completely transformed – from the teaching methods and resources used, to the range of material studied, and the subject-knowledge and professionalism of teachers. All these advances should, over time, lead to considerable improvements in literacy standards, particularly if teachers are now given time to consolidate what they have learned, and are trusted to move their practice forward.

However, the transformation has not been without its difficulties. Too often the short-term interests of politicians have been allowed to override the long-term interests of the children for whom the Strategy was devised. Many schools and teachers have felt pressurised into coaching and 'boosting' for national tests, rather than properly putting new ideas into practice. At its worst this has led to arid and joyless literacy lessons – and, therefore, limited learning.

In spring 2003, the Literacy Strategy was subsumed by the National Primary Strategy which, in its introductory document, *Excellence and Enjoyment*, promised more emphasis on how children learn and on encouraging teachers' ownership of literacy teaching. We welcome these developments, and hope this summary of what *we've* learned (and thoughts on where literacy teaching should go next) may be of help as the profession takes its next steps along the road to universal literacy.

- The Framework, searchlights and Literacy Hour   6
- The teaching of reading   8
- The teaching of writing   10
- Key teaching strategies   12
- Where do we go next?   14

The Framework, the Searchlights and the Literacy Hour

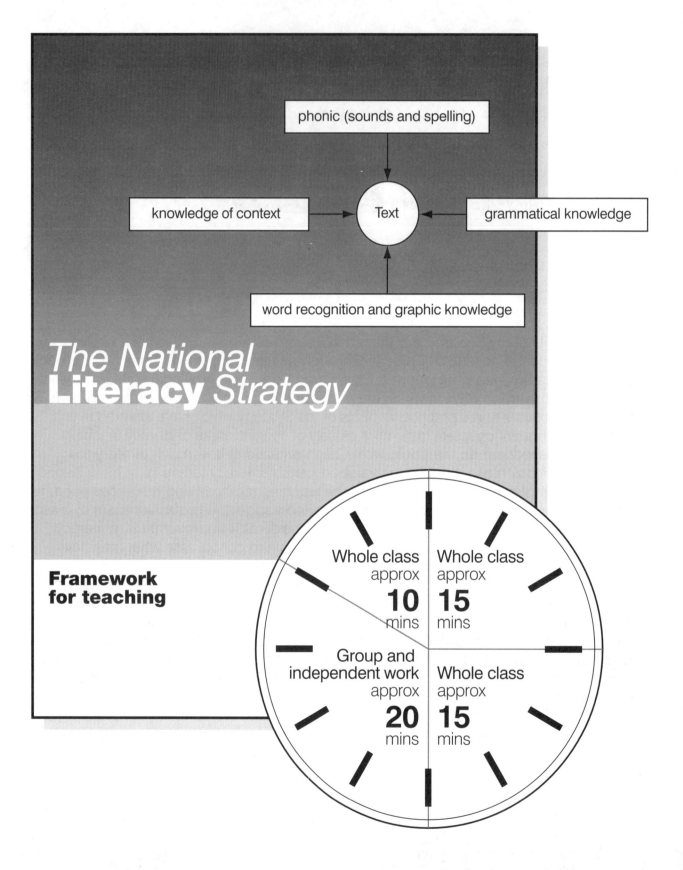

The Framework of teaching objectives

This comprehensive summary of teaching objectives has had a profound effect upon literacy teaching, summed up by a teacher in the first year of the Strategy:

> *I used to think 'Well, here's a lovely book – what shall I do with it?'. Now I think, 'Right, here's what I've got to do – where can I find a lovely book to help me do it?'*

After an initial period of dismay, teachers everywhere welcomed this list of 'what to do'. They have also learned to stick to the spirit of the document rather than the letter. Whereas, in the early days, the term-by-term order of teaching was followed rigidly, many teachers now feel knowledgeable and confident enough to swap objectives around to fit their own school circumstances.

Another advantage of the Framework is that it encourages a collegiate approach. Literacy teaching is such an enormous and complex business that it must be seen as an on-going process, starting in reception (or preferably before) and continuing throughout Key Stages 1, 2 and 3 and beyond. The Framework ensures that all teachers are clear about their own and others' contribution to this collegiate endeavour. It has also developed a shared vocabulary of teaching terms, helpful to both teachers and pupils.

The Searchlight Model

Although some academics dislike the searchlight model upon which the Strategy is based, we have found it exceptionally helpful. It shows very clearly that the getting of literacy is a complex process, involving the orchestration of many skills. The division of these skills into word, sentence and text level skills is inspired, and has greatly clarified teachers' thinking and practice. Chapter 2 of this book considers major issues that have arisen at word level, Chapter 3 at sentence level and Chapters 4 and 5 at text level.

The Literacy Hour

This most controversial element of the NLS was intended to ensure that every teacher:

- devoted at least one hour a day of ring-fenced time to literacy;
- used shared, guided and independent teaching methods, plus a plenary session;
- established a more structured, systematic approach to their teaching.

Six years on, it is probably fair to say that it was a sledgehammer to crack a nut. Most teachers would have embraced all these principles with enthusiasm and, given more freedom to implement them, might well have got to grips with the underlying ideas of the Strategy more quickly. Indeed, in Wales, where the Strategy was not imposed, practice has changed just as much and standards risen just as quickly – without the element of demoralisation that the Literacy Hour brought in many English schools.

The Literacy Hour was, in fact, more to do with policy than pedagogy. It grabbed the headlines, it was a useful medium for the biggest national retraining programme of all time, and it was easy to check up on (in the early days some Ofsted inspectors expected almost military precision). However, in schools where it was managed well, it provided a useful starting point, especially for new or unconfident staff. One young teacher compared it to 'base camp': once she knew her way around she could set off on exploratory forays up the mountain, secure that she could return to base at any time. Sadly in other schools there was all sorts of nonsense – from stopclocks and egg-timers to the imposition of massive photocopiable 'schemes'.

Many schools have now, mercifully, abandoned the rigid timing of the Literacy Hour, whilst sticking to its fundamental principles. Where it is retained, we hope it is in the 'base camp' spirit.

The Teaching of Reading

What are we teaching?

- **the basic skills for reading** e.g. using the 'searchlights', fluency, reading on, predicting;

- **techniques to navigate texts** e.g. skimming, scanning, using topic sentences as clues, information retrieval, visualising, predicting;

- **comprehension strategies** e.g. speculating, deducing, inferring, interpreting, making connections, authorial intent;

- **developing responses** e.g. likes, dislikes, puzzles, questioning, re-evaluating, connecting with own experience, empathising, referring to text to support views, considering overall impact.

NLS teaching sequence for reading

- **Preparation** – decide what reading strategy/behaviour or objective needs teaching.

- **Demonstrate reading** – explain strategy and specifically demonstrate, giving a running commentary on what you are doing.

- **Shared reading** – now the children attempt using the strategy, with the teacher prompting.

- **Independent/supported/guided reading** – children practise using the same strategy, with support where necessary.

Developing an approach to reading

From the very beginning, the major thrust of the National Literacy Strategy was a focus on improving children's reading. The introduction of *Progression in Phonics* was a major breakthrough as it helped teachers clarify the effective teaching of phonics – as both knowledge (which letter/s represent what sounds) and skills (blending for reading and segmenting for writing). The National Literacy Strategy also introduced two key techniques to the nation – shared and guided reading. Thus began a revolution.

Shared reading

In shared reading the teacher, as expert reader, demonstrates reading strategies using a shared text. The text should be at a level that would not normally be read by the class so that there is an edge of challenge. The publishing of Big Books and OHTs (and more recently interactive whiteboards) had a massive impact on classroom practice. It became the 'easy' part of the hour. Many teachers and children enjoyed the breadth of reading.

Unfortunately, where teachers lacked confidence and subject knowledge, instead of carefully considering what reading strategy might need to be taught and demonstrating this, shared reading remained at a superficial level. The class read the text together (some mouthing words like goldfish) with the teacher helping! Then the teacher asked a few questions before the children went off and did some work. At least this meant the children were doing more regular reading than before, but it weakened the Strategy's impact.

Training for literacy consultants in 2002 attempted to address this issue, as it became apparent that the rise of standards in reading had ground to a halt. The training provided a more direct model for teaching, based on the teaching sequence for writing. It involves deciding what reading strategy needs teaching, demonstrating how this is done, and prompting the class to use the strategy before they practise independently.

Guided reading

Guided reading initially caused much controversy as it was suggested that this would take the place of hearing individuals read. Many schools maintained some hearing of reading, especially in reception classes and with those who were struggling. Others provided support through daily lunchtime reading clubs for those who were not getting help at home.

In guided reading, a group works on a carefully selected text that offers an appropriate level of challenge for that group. Reading strategies are discussed and the group reads, followed by a discussion. The teacher supports and prompts the children to apply the strategies, promoting independent reading. The focus for young readers is usually on decoding, whilst more mature readers will spend time interrogating the text, inferring and deducing. Again, guided reading is not yet used by every school and in many classes it remains at the level of 'round robin reading'.

Independent reading

As well as being taught to read, children also need many opportunities to read for themselves. In the early stages, they need plenty of practice to develop strategies and fluency; later, there should be time to read for pleasure, personal enrichment and information (see Appendix 3 for suggestions on promoting reading).

Independent reading may be an individual pursuit, occur during the literacy lesson or some other designated time in the classroom, or be supervised by parents for homework. On page 67 we suggest paired reading, providing an opportunity to read aloud. There may also be times when groups can read independently of the teacher, perhaps dramatising a play script or devising the presentation of a poem or piece of prose.

The Teaching of Writing

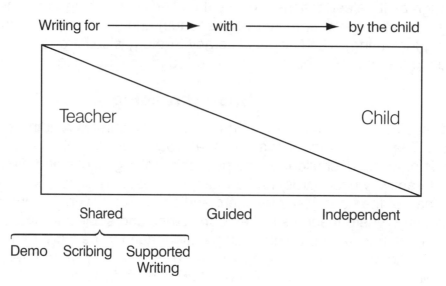

NLS teaching sequence for writing

Develop writer's knowledge:

1. read good quality examples

2. teach specific text/sentence level objectives

3. summarise what's been learned about the text type ('toolkit', checklist)

Develop writing skill:

4. prepare and plan

5. shared writing
   - demonstration – teacher models process
   - shared composition – teacher scribes and edits
   - supported writing – whiteboard work

6. independent (or guided) writing

7. publish and review

Developing an approach to writing

Writing was pinpointed as a problem area in 1998, when national test results showed significant underachievement, especially for boys. The NLS, which had so far paid rather more attention to the teaching of reading, immediately began targeting writing.

A series of fliers in 1999 provided a model for 'shared, guided and independent writing' in which control of the writing process passes gradually from teacher to pupil, as shown in the diagram opposite. These also advised devoting two or three shared sessions a week to writing. In 2000 KS2 teachers received copies of *Grammar for Writing*, emphasising sentence level work (see Chapter 3), and in 2002 *Developing Early Writing* was sent to KS1 teachers. By this time attention had turned to the importance of planning and 'talk for writing', stressed in that same year in a series of 'text level' fliers (see Chapters 4 and 5).

There has therefore been notable development in the Strategy's approach to writing over time, and the Teaching Sequence opposite is the latest in a long line of such sequences, each more complex than the last. While it's always been recognised that writing is best addressed in series of lessons, linked to similar series of lessons on reading the text-type, the NLS has only recently stressed the importance of links to other curricular areas, including the arts.

Shared writing

The introduction of shared writing provided teachers with a means of directly teaching the writing process – rather than merely enthusing children to write and responding to their writing. While these two elements are still important (they are included in the Teaching Sequence opposite and dealt with at more length in Chapters 4 and 5), we have not in the past paid enough attention to what is involved in the actual act of composition. The shared writing model attempts to cover:

- **demonstration**: the teacher models the process of composition, providing a running commentary on what's happening at a level appropriate to the class, and with specific reference to the teaching objective of the day;
- **shared composition**: pupils join in composing with the teacher as editor and scribe, keeping the focus clearly on the objective and encouraging oral rehearsal of sentences;
- **supported writing**: pupils work on whiteboards on focused writing tasks related to the objective, with supportive strategies, e.g. writing partners, writing frames.

Independent writing

This should follow immediately after shared writing, the major writing objective(s) should be clear, and adequate support provided (e.g. checklists and 'writer's toolkits' compiled during preparation). Some children may require further scaffolding in the form of writing frames, model texts, sentence starts and so on. There should be established classroom routines for dealing with problems such as checking for a spelling (see Chapter 2).

Guided writing

While pupils are writing independently, the teacher may work with a specific group. This may be an ability group, needing further support to achieve the objective or greater challenge to address it at a higher level – sometime this may turn into 'guided talk'. Occasionally, it might be an ad hoc group of children all of whom need to concentrate on a specific area, such as sentence punctuation or direct speech. Teaching a group rather than individuals helps teachers concentrate on the objective rather than a specific child's work. This means children – especially younger or less able children – are encouraged to take responsibility for their writing for themselves, instead of developing dependency on the teacher.

Key Teaching Strategies

Interactivity in the shared session

Show Me
e.g. whiteboards, letter fans, actions

Shared and paired work
(see 'talking partners', page 59)

Get Up And Go
learning through movement

Drama
e.g. role-play, hotseating, freeze-framing (see Appendix 1)

Investigative strategies

investigating aspects of language use in real texts

Interactivity in the plenary session

What did we learn?
e.g. talking partners, checklists

Group presentations
e.g. oral reports of investigations, presentations of poems or stories

Games
e.g. Any Questions, Countdown, Shannon's Game, based on the day's objectives

Literacy: what works? © Sue Palmer and Pie Corbett, Nelson Thornes, 2003

Interactivity in the shared session

The NLS has always stressed that shared work does not mean old-fashioned chalk and talk, and in some 1999 fliers suggested ways to involve all children, not just the usual half dozen who put their hands up. **Show Me** activities, in which all answer at once (silently!), are now widespread – indeed, the individual whiteboard has become as ubiquitous as its forerunner, the slate. Children could also devise suitable actions – for, say, a variety of spelling patterns – thus drawing on the kinaesthetic learning channel as well.

The **talking partner** technique (see page 59), allows you to intersperse shared teaching with questions or tasks for children to consider in pairs. This ensures that everyone engages with the question – because they don't know whom you'll ask to feed back.

Get Up And Go means activities involving movement, such as rearranging letters, words or clauses on a washing line or making 'human sentences'. Most children benefit greatly from kinaesthetic learning – and from regular occasions to move a little during the lesson. Punctuating teaching with short bursts of activity, such as making actions for a spelling pattern (e.g. *OK, we'll break for a minute and just do a couple of our words*), refocuses children's attention while delivering a quick fix of oxygen to their brains.

Drama activities also involve movement, and can be a marvellous way to explore character and motivation. But don't stop there – what about role-playing the punctuation marks (decide on characters for each and give them names) or asking children to devise a short playlet to explain a spelling pattern?

Investigative strategies

There is one thing of which we are both certain: grammar and spelling worksheets don't teach grammar and spelling. Unfortunately they are widespread during the independent section of the hour. We can't understand why most independent time isn't consumed by 'real' reading and writing activities, but when word and sentence follow-up are required, investigations (using real texts) are far preferable to worksheets. They are easy to set up, don't need a photocopier, expand to fill the given time, scarcely need marking and can be differentiated for age and ability – so they're much less bother than worksheets too.

The simplest task is just to find examples of the language feature under consideration (less able pupils could use highlighting tape to mark up examples for you to use in the plenary). The next level up is to collect and sort according to criteria given by you – e.g. *Find apostrophes and sort into two columns headed 'Omission' and 'Possession'*. The most demanding task is for pairs of children to collect, discuss and work out criteria for use, all by themselves.

The plenary session

In their 2000 review of the NLS Ofsted recommended the use of the plenary session to:

- reinforce the learning objectives of the lesson;
- feed back to pupils to show them what they had to do to improve;
- use pupils' contributions – e.g. evaluations of their own and others' work;
- make links between what pupils have done and work in other areas of the curriculum;
- provide homework, where appropriate, to extend what has been learned.

Given its usefulness, we are surprised that the plenary is not universally used – if not at the end of each lesson, at least at regular intervals during a sequence of lessons.

The more children are involved in the plenary the better. For instance, talking partners can be asked to *Think of the three most important things we've learned today* or to fill in a checklist of objectives on a piece of displayed work. Individuals, pairs or groups can be briefed that they are presenting in plenary today (and perhaps given a checklist in advance, to ensure they keep focused). The more opportunities we can provide for children to articulate what they have learned, the better they will retain it.

Where Do We Go Next?

Learn from the past

The National Primary Strategy is, like its predecessor, a centralised government-funded agency, and will come under the same political pressures. We hope it will not repeat major errors made by the NLS due to political interference:

1. Too much too soon
The speed with which politicians required the NLS to be introduced caused many problems, for instance:

- teachers were expected to introduce the Literacy Hour and objectives before they had completed the training, leading to overwork, loss of confidence, and many misconceptions;
- Strategy materials were often produced at speed with inadequate trialling (and, embarrassingly, with incorrect grammatical definitions and spelling mistakes);
- money for schools to spend on books was made available before publishers could produce them, so much was wasted on shoddy, ill-conceived or inappropriate materials.

2. Accountability and bureaucracy are not the same thing
Ofsted's obsession with planning in the early days of the Strategy resulted in widespread professional paranoia. Many teachers still spend so much of their time filling in planning sheets and copying out teaching objectives that they have no time, energy or enthusiasm left for teaching.

3. Too much pressure; the wrong kind of support
The tests and targets agenda used to kick-start the literacy drive (and to persuade the Treasury to part with funds) led to pressure for ever-higher SAT results, so that many schools began focusing narrowly on the skills required for these tests, at the expense of a broad and balanced curriculum. The NLS compounded this uncreative approach to teaching by producing 'planning exemplification materials' (which look suspiciously like scripted lessons), further encouraging the climate of prescriptiveness.

Look at Wales

While English teachers struggled with the Literacy Hour, Welsh teachers were encouraged to raise standards in a more reasonable way. The Welsh authorities cherry-picked the best of the NLS, gave their teachers longer to introduce changes, and involved the profession more in this process of change. While NLS directives descended on schools like holy writ, Estyn, the Welsh equivalent of Ofsted, published 'discussion documents'. Because they listen to teachers, the Welsh are now streets ahead of England in dealing with the main problem areas of targets, testing and the over-formality of Early Years.

Trust teachers

Contrary to the opinion of Chris Woodhead and some sections of the press, the overwhelming majority of teachers are hard-working, sensible, intelligent people, committed to doing the best for the children in their care. Where they have failed in raising literacy standards in the past, it has been the result of inadequate accountability, bad advice and/or poor leadership. However, Ofsted and national testing now ensure that schools are fully accountable, the NLS has provided a great deal of good advice, and the NPS is committed to strengthening our schools' leadership. Now, surely, it's time to trust the profession to get on with the job.

Phonics, Handwriting and Spelling

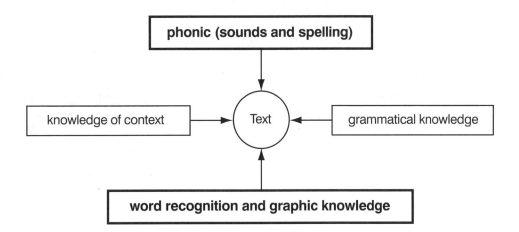

In the NLS 'searchlight' model, two major searchlights relate to word level skills. In order to read, young children must learn to draw on phonic knowledge to decode regularly spelled words, switching to whole-word recognition when they encounter irregularly spelled words (which are rather common in English). However, the remaining two searchlights offer the reader considerable extra support, and it is possible to read at a basic level with incomplete or shaky phonic knowledge.

Writing, however, requires much greater control of word level skills. In order to write, a child must be able to:

- discriminate individual speech sounds (phonemes) in a word;
- convert these into written symbols (graphemes);
- remember these phoneme-grapheme correspondences in the correct order;
- transcribe them on to the page; **and**
- remember, and swap tactics for, those common irregularly spelled words which must be processed as 'wholes'.

In addition, writing requires a further skill: the manipulation of a pencil over the paper to create recognisable symbols. We therefore believe that in the early stages explicit word level teaching is much more significant for writing than for reading.

As time goes on, both spelling and handwriting must become automatic if children are to write successfully – the child that is struggling with these basic skills has no room left in its head for the higher order skills of composition. Thorough teaching of word level skills is therefore fundamental to children's long term success as writers.

- What teachers need to know about phonics   16
- Key points for teaching phonics   18
- Teaching handwriting   20
- Spelling by eye, ear, hand and brain   22
- Day-to-day spelling   24
- Where do we go next?   26

What Teachers Need to Know About Phonics

The phonemes of English

and some common ways of representing them

Consonant phonemes with consistent spellings

/b/	**b**at, ra**bb**it
/d/	**d**og, da**dd**y
/g/	**g**irl, gi**gg**le
/h/	**h**ot
/l/	**l**og, lo**ll**y
/m/	**m**at, su**mm**er
/n/	**n**ut, di**nn**er
/p/	**p**ig, su**pp**er
/r/	**r**at, ca**rr**y
/t/	**t**op, pa**tt**er
/y/	**y**ellow
/th/	**th**is (voiced) **th**ing (unvoiced)

Consonant phonemes with alternative spellings

/k/	**c**at, **k**ing, ba**ck**, s**ch**ool, **qu**een (also the /k/ sound in bo**x**)
/s/	**s**un, pre**ss**, **c**ircle
/f/	**f**un, **ph**oto
/j/	**j**am, **g**inger, bri**dge**
/w/	**w**orm, q**u**een
/z/	**z**oo, pin**s**, **x**ylophone
/v/	**v**an (one exception: o**f**)
/sh/	**sh**eep, sta**ti**on, **ch**ef
/ch/	**ch**in, i**tch**
/ng/	si**ng**, pi**n**k
/zh/	mea**s**ure, a**z**ure

'Short' and 'long' vowel phonemes

/a/	b**a**g
/e/	b**e**t, br**ea**d, s**ai**d
/i/	b**i**g, c**y**linder
/o/	t**o**p, w**a**s
/u/	b**u**n, l**o**ve
/ae/	d**ay**, p**ai**n, g**a**t**e**, gr**ea**t
/ee/	f**ee**t, s**ea**t, P**e**t**e**, m**e**
/ie/	t**ie**, t**igh**t, fl**y**, t**i**m**e**
/oa/	b**oa**t, gr**ow**, b**o**n**e**, t**oe**, g**o**
/ue/	bl**ue**, m**oo**n, gr**ew**, fl**u**t**e**, y**ou**

Other vowel phonemes

/oo/	g**oo**d, p**u**t, c**ou**ld, w**o**lf
/ur/	ch**ur**ch, b**ir**d, h**er**b, **ear**th, w**or**d
/ar/	st**ar**t, f**a**ther
/or/	c**or**n, d**oor**, sh**ore**, r**oar**, y**our**
/aw/	p**aw**, t**au**t, t**a**ll, t**a**lk, t**augh**t
/ow/	cl**ow**n, sh**ou**t
/oy/	b**oy**, **oi**l
/ear/	n**ear**, d**eer**, h**ere**
/air/	ch**air**, sh**are**, th**ere**
'schwa' (see opposite)	farm**er**, doct**or**, gramm**ar**, met**re**, col**our**, Americ**a** ...

The NLS suggests teachers introduce one way of writing each phoneme (i.e. the first spelling pattern given in each list of examples). Later, other main spelling patterns can be introduced, widening the spelling choices.

Literacy: what works? © Sue Palmer and Pie Corbett, Nelson Thornes, 2003

The 'reading wars' of the last century involved more skirmishes about phonics than anything else. The subject seems to attract extremists and obsessives – teachers should be cautious about whom and what they believe on the subject. However, two facts seem clear:

- 'phonemic awareness' (the insight that you can split up a word like *dog* into individual speech sounds and blend it together again) and a working knowledge of the 'alphabet code' by which we represent speech sounds seem critical to success in both reading and writing;
- given that the English language is about 80% phonetically regular, all teachers should have a working knowledge of phonics for the teaching of spelling.

Useful technical vocabulary

phoneme	individual speech sound
CVC word	consonant-vowel-consonant word, e.g. *dog*
	CVC words are the simplest type of words to decode or encode.
segmenting and blending	taking a word apart into its individual phonemes (e.g. /c/ /a//t/) and putting it back together ('cat'). A child's ability to do this seems to be fundamental to the development of literacy skills.
consonant cluster	two or more consonant phonemes, e.g. *twig* (CCVC), *lunch* (CVCC), *splash* (CCCVC). In the past such letter-groups were often called 'blends'. However, the NLS changed the terminology because 'blending' is now used in another important context (see above).
digraph	two letters standing for one phoneme, e.g. *sh*, *ay*
trigraph	three letters standing for one phoneme, e.g. *igh*, *ear*
onset and rime	in a single syllable word, the onset is the part of the word that comes before the vowel (**c**at; **gr**and, **str**ong); the rime is the vowel and the rest of the word (c**at**; gr**and**; str**ong**). Once a child is able to blend and segment words easily, it is helpful to look at words in terms of larger units – first, onset and rime; later, syllables.
split digraph	a long vowel phoneme involving final silent **e**, e.g. *gate, Pete, time, bone, flute*. In the past this was often called 'magic e' – NLS introduced this terminology because the vowel sound is represented by a digraph (as in *tie*) which has been split up by another letter (as in *time*).
schwa	an indeterminate grunting sound. The schwa is the most common vowel sound in the English language, and uncertainty about how to represent it is behind many common spelling errors, e.g. *seperate* (separate), *definately* (definitely).
morpheme	a unit of meaning, often related to grammatical function (e.g. *–ed, -tion, -ly*). Morphemes are important elements in reading and spelling, and often they are not phonetically consistent, e.g. *–ed* represents a different sound in *jumped, listened, wanted*.

Key Points for Teaching Phonics

1. Go from **sound** to **symbol** (not the other way about).

2. Teach phonic **skills** as well as phonic **knowledge**.

3. Make your teaching **fun**, **fast**, **multisensory** and **cumulative**.

4. Teach phonics **daily**, **systematically** and **relentlessly**!

5. Don't worry if children don't remember a sound or skill first time... or second... or third...

6. Ensure a clear structure for teaching – including frequent and regular revision.

7. Demonstrate how to **use** phonics during shared reading and writing.

8. As time goes on, link phonics to handwriting.

9. As time goes further on, widen teaching to involve other spelling strategies.

10. Provide extra help for stragglers.

Literacy: what works? © Sue Palmer and Pie Corbett, Nelson Thornes, 2003

1. First make sure children can hear the phoneme (e.g. by using the *Jolly Phonics* technique of associating each phoneme with an action, which can be used for games – *I say the sound, you make the action* and vice versa). Then introduce one way of writing it (see page 16). Later, when you know the sound is well-established, you can widen the spelling choices.

2. From the very beginning, use games that illustrate how to blend and segment simple words (e.g. *I'm going to talk like a robot who can only say sounds. Who can tell me what **word** the robot's trying to say? C-A-T*). It's important that children don't get hung up on initial sounds. They also need to develop auditory memory for sound sequences.

3. Phonics – like all language skills – is not in itself interesting to children. It is therefore up to us to motivate them by making teaching methods child-friendly, fun and memorable. Aim for activities that are short and punchy, to which you can return time and again. Try to involve all the sensory channels: auditory, visual, articulatory, kinaesthetic, tactile (and, wherever possible, the sense of humour).

4. Until phonic skills and knowledge are established, aim to teach them specifically for fifteen to twenty minutes every day (not necessarily in a single block). In addition, use phonic games and songs as time-fillers for odd minutes here and there, in the dinner queue, waiting for assembly... Keep coming back, again and again...

5. We repeatedly hear successful teachers say *I just kept on doing it, over and over, and suddenly they got it!*

6. Structure, system and good record-keeping are essential. You might use the NLS's *Progression in Phonics*, an adaptation of it, or a commercial scheme. Whatever scheme you adopt, you'll probably want to augment the activities with other ideas from elsewhere. But to ensure systematic coverage (and for your own sanity), stick to a set order of teaching, incorporating continual revision, and keep clear records of what each child has learned.

7. The point of teaching all these skills and knowledge is to use them in reading and writing. Take every opportunity to demonstrate explicitly how phonics can be used during shared work – there is an excellent illustration of a reception teacher doing this on the NLS *Developing Early Writing* video, distributed to all English schools in 2001.

8. Once children have developed the physical skills and control to write comfortably, one obvious kinaesthetic teaching strategy is to link recognition of sounds to formation of letters and groups of letters through handwriting and dictation (see page 21).

9. Once basic phonic skills and knowledge are established, take care that pupils do not become over-dependent on them as a spelling strategy. By Year 2 most children should be developing a range of spelling strategies to use alongside phonics for writing (see page 22).

10. No matter how good the teaching, there will always be some children who do not catch on. Try to identify such children as soon as possible (look out for more than usual difficulty in remembering phoneme-grapheme correspondences and, particularly, in segmenting and blending words), and provide extra support. For many children the NLS's *Early Learning Support* programme provides a useful safety net, but others may need more sustained and structured support – see page 95 for sources of information on dyslexia.

Teaching Handwriting

the curly caterpillar

c

Start at the caterpillar's head,
Come back round,
under his tummy...
and curl up for his tail.

the long ladder

l

Start at the top,
go DOWN the long ladder,
and flick up at the end.

the one-armed robot

r

Start at the robot's head,
go down his body,
back up his body,
and over for his robot
arm.

c group: c a d g o qu s   l group: l t i u y j

r group: r n m h k p b   others: e f v w x z

tall letters: d h b l k (t)

short letters: a c e o m n i r s u v w x z

letters with tails: f g y j p qu

letters that join from the top: o v w

consonant digraphs: th ch sh

basic long vowels: ay ee ie oa oo

other long vowel joins: ai ea igh ow ue ew or ar er

ir ur oy oi aw au ear air

high frequency words for joining:

he	the	my	or	come	one	was
she	they	you	for	some	gone	went
me	them	your	are	said	done	want
the	there	our				

Literacy: what works? © Sue Palmer and Pie Corbett, Nelson Thornes, 2003

Preparation for handwriting

We have considerable reservations about the NLS's requirement that all children have to learn to write the alphabet letter shapes during the reception year. At the age of four or five, some children – especially boys – have not developed the necessary hand-eye co-ordination and fine motor control for this complex task. There is a strong possibility that by asking very young children to write before they are ready, we are setting them up to fail, with disastrous long-term effects. We should like to see much more time devoted to preparatory activities before formal handwriting tuition is introduced (see also page 80).

Preparation for handwriting should involve large-scale motor movements (e.g. dance, drama), activities to develop the muscles of the fingers (e.g. finger-rhymes) and hand-eye co-ordination (e.g. cutting, threading, drawing). There are many useful suggestions in the *Penpals Foundation 1* materials (CUP), leading towards the formation of the three major handwriting shapes suggested by the NLS: the curly caterpillar, the long ladder and the one-armed robot. These three shapes underlie most letter formations.

Initial teaching

When formal teaching begins, children should practise shapes first as a large motor movement (extended arm, moving from the shoulder), then in 'skywriting' with a finger in the air, before finally writing with pen on whiteboard or pencil on paper. Many children find it helps to chant a consistent 'jingle' or commentary as they form the letter. Letter shapes are best practised in groups which share a similar formation. This is a good opportunity to revise sound-symbol correspondences already learned through auditory and visual channels.

Our experience suggests that very young children find it easier to learn to form letters individually in the early stages. Given that we start writing so early in Britain, we would not recommend teaching 'joined up writing' (sometimes called 'cursive script') from the beginning. However, if children are taught to write letters with 'flicks' – as in the popular Nelson Handwriting style illustrated opposite – they are ready to join as soon as possible.*

We like the idea of using handwriting to consolidate phonic knowledge, by joining common digraphs from an early stage. This could begin with the joining of the three consonant digraphs and the basic spellings of the long vowel phonemes, so that pupils learn to associate a single movement and a joined shape with each common digraph. As further spellings of vowel digraphs and trigraphs are covered, these too could be taught as handwriting 'wholes'. Similarly, as soon as children are competent to do so, they could learn to join some of the high frequency words which must also be remembered as wholes.

Handwriting practice

It is important to establish a good foundation in handwriting in Key Stage 1. In Key Stage 2, regular lessons should continue – little and often is best – preferably linked to the teaching of spelling. Children who develop a neat, flowing hand are liberated to write easily and speedily. Schemes (e.g. *Nelson Handwriting*, CUP's *Penpals*) can provide a structure.

At all levels teaching should target speed and fluency (sometimes using blank paper) and size, orientation, letter-formation and joins (always using lined paper). Whiteboards, blank on one side and lined on the other, are ideal for short dictation lessons in KS1 – starting with single phonemes and building up to CVC words and eventually simple sentences. Dictation allows children to concentrate exclusively on skills of sound recognition and transcription, and is also ideal for spelling/handwriting practice at the appropriate level throughout KS2.

* Where children have plenty of time for preparation, as in the French *Graphisme* programme, joined writing is possible from the start.

Spelling by Eye, Ear, Hand and Brain

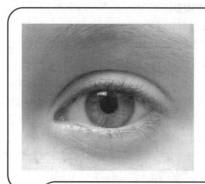

Find the tricky bit and highlight it.

Watch out for words within words.

Take special note of double letters.

Watch out for common letterstrings.

separate
soldier
happened
thought
enough

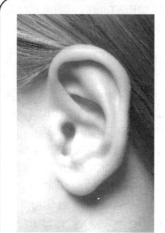

Use rhyme.

Seg-ment words in-to syll-ab-les.

Ex-agg-**er**-**a**te the pr**o**-nun-ci-**a**-tio**n**

(**e**s-p**e**-ci-**a**ll-y the v**ow**-**e**ls).

Pronounce silent letters and silent syllables (e.g. lis**t**en, Wed**nes**day).

Chant the letters, e.g. Q-UE-UE.

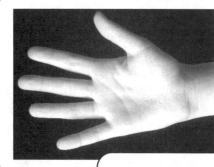

Link an action to the chant.

Practise tricky words in joined writing. Get as fast as you can.

Write the word with your finger in the air, a stick in the sand, a water-squirter on the ground...

Watch out for families of words: *medicine, medical, medic.*

Remember rules and conventions: *i before e, except after c.*

Work out what seems most likely.

If all else fails, make up an mnemonic. *Never be**lie**ve a lie.*

LOOK   SAY   COVER   WRITE   CHECK

(and think!) (and listen!)

Literacy: what works? © Sue Palmer and Pie Corbett, Nelson Thornes, 2003

Teaching spelling is about alerting children to **patterns**:

- patterns of sounds and letters, such as onset and rime;
- patterns relating to grammatical function, such as common suffixes;
- patterns relating to word origins, such as the link between *sign* and *signal*.

In order to study words in this way, we have to take them out of context. This means devoting a little time each day to specific teaching of spelling.

However, awareness of patterns and rules is not enough. Mastery of the English spelling system also requires the marshalling of sensory information through visual, auditory and kinaesthetic channels. Some children are stronger in one area than another, but all benefit from learning and regularly revising the full range of spelling strategies.

For these reasons, spelling must be actively **taught**. The traditional workbook exercises, wordlists and spelling tests are not enough: children need explicit interactive teaching which draws their attention to the shape and sounds of words, the letter patterns within them, and the various ways they can remember these patterns.

Such teaching need not take long – the secret of successful teaching of spelling is 'little and often'. The NLS framework of objectives provides lists of rules and patterns to be introduced in each term. For each of these, teaching should involve:

- drawing up a list of relevant words, especially high frequency words and ones which have relevance to pupils' current work and interest (this can often be the focus of a 'spelling investigation', where pupils hunt for appropriate words);
- focus on the specific spelling point (e.g. a grammatical rule, a letter-string, some aspect of etymology) so that pupils clearly understand the pattern;
- concentration on some significant words from the list, drawing on – and thus revising – a range of strategies for learning and remembering spellings (see opposite page);
- opportunities for pupils to practise recently learned words in context – short dictation passages provide an opportunity for them to focus just on transcription skills, without the added burden of composition.

As well as the NLS's *Spelling Bank*, there are now a number of published schemes which cover the NLS requirements, including Pie's *Searchlights for Spelling* (CUP) and Sue's *Ginn Big Book Spelling*. These provide ready-made lessons, lists of appropriate words and dictation passages.

Supporting the poor speller

Spelling is an area where differentiation is particularly important. For a child who has not yet grasped basic phonics satisfactorily, joining in with class work on the suffix *tion* (with its emphasis on long, complex words) will probably do more harm than good. Poor spellers can be involved along with the rest of the class in learning spelling strategies, preferably focusing on commonly misspelled high frequency words, but teachers should exercise judgement on whether other spelling work would be detrimental.

If so, spelling time might be better spent on an individualised programme appropriate to the child's own level. There are a number of interactive computer courses, such as *Wordshark*, which provide very structured help, but poor spellers really need specialised teaching. The solution to the knotty problem of providing it will necessarily be up to individual teachers in individual schools, with the involvement of the SENCO.

Day-to-day Spelling

Have a go!

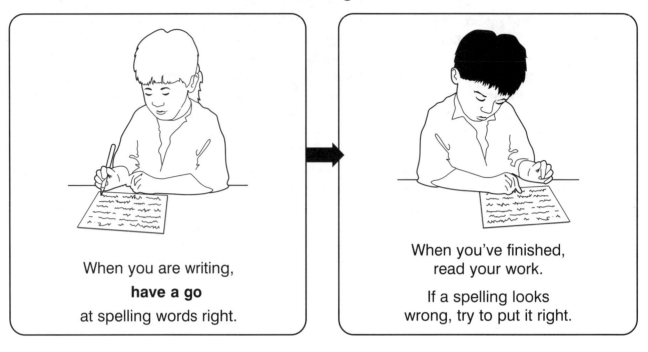

When you are writing,
have a go
at spelling words right.

When you've finished,
read your work.

If a spelling looks
wrong, try to put it right.

Proof-reading for Spelling

As you read through your work, underline misspelled words in pensel.
(You could also do this as you write.)

When you're checking your work, come back to these
words one at a time:
- have another go at each word on scrap paper –
- if it looks right, correct it in the text
- if you're still unsure, try

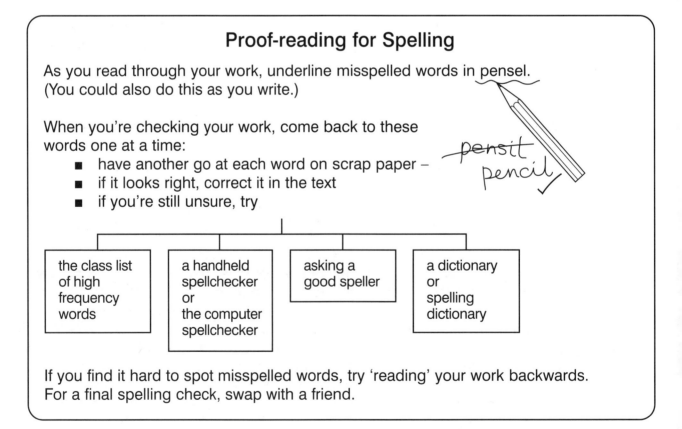

| the class list of high frequency words | a handheld spellchecker or the computer spellchecker | asking a good speller | a dictionary or spelling dictionary |

If you find it hard to spot misspelled words, try 'reading' your work backwards.
For a final spelling check, swap with a friend.

Day-to-day spelling

Regular phonics activities and, later, spelling lessons are the opportunity to provide children with essential data about the way words are constructed. But frequent opportunities to write – for engaging and meaningful reasons – provide the opportunity to use this data, and by using it, to consolidate learning.

However, there is much more involved in writing than spelling, and when actually writing children should be concentrating on these higher order skills – generating and organising content, composing sentences, choosing effective vocabulary.

As far as spelling is concerned, they should simply '**have a go**'. You can model this 'having a go' during shared writing by 'thinking aloud' as you encode a tricky word, showing how spelling knowledge and strategies are marshalled during the act of writing, but not letting it interfere with your composition. Similarly, when children are writing encourage them to draw on what they have learned and orchestrate the skills, but without getting bogged down in worrying about spelling. The time to worry about spelling is when they are reviewing their work, either at the end or during a natural break in the composition.

Provide a simple **proof-reading guide**, giving a routine for checking and correcting spelling, and train children to use it so that it becomes second nature. Integrate this with a clear marking policy (see Chapter 7).

Supporting the poor speller during writing

Children who have difficulties with spelling need extra support. One thing they should know is that some people are just rotten spellers, and spelling problems should not inhibit them from writing. As far as possible, they too should 'have a go', but if this means they repeatedly misspell common words (e.g. *thay* or *sed*), they will overlearn the incorrect spelling. During writing, therefore, provide instant access to high-frequency commonly misspelled words via:

- a wall chart of commonly misspelled words;
- a small personal dictionary (small address books, with alphabetised pages, are useful for this);
- a 'spelling mat' on which the words are written in alphabetical lists, and which the child leans on to write (this is the best option as the child does not have to lift its head from the writing task, and is thus less likely to break its train of thought).

In all cases, the pupil can share the general instruction to 'have a go', but with an important proviso: *Have a go – unless it's on your list. If it's on your list, copy it correctly.* This provides the opportunity to over-learn the **correct** spelling.

By Year 5, spelling difficulties can seriously inhibit composition. It is important – but very difficult – to balance the need for remedial help in spelling lessons (extra practice to automatise spelling of NLS high-frequency words can make a huge cosmetic difference) with the need to minimise pupils' concentration on spelling during writing. Many children benefit from learning to use handheld electronic spellcheckers, which often free poor spellers to experiment with more sophisticated vocabulary and which, as long as they don't contain a thesaurus, may be taken into the writing SAT. Since these now cost less than £20 it may be possible to provide one for each poor speller. See also reference to tablet PCs and speech recognition software (page 26).

Where Do We Go Next?

Revise policy on Early Years

In other European countries, formal teaching of literacy skills does not begin till children are 6 or 7 years old. Instead, time is spent on child-centred preparatory activities, particularly the development of speaking and listening abilities and physical skills required for fluent handwriting. Wales is about to follow suit, introducing a new extended Foundation Stage.

In England, however, the National Curriculum begins in Year 1, when most children are just 5, and due to our obsessive tests and targets culture, formal learning has found its way increasingly into reception classes – sometimes even nurseries. Some children from very advantaged backgrounds may be ready to start formal learning at 4 or even 3 years old (although we would question whether it does them much good overall). However, many children, especially boys, would benefit more from the sort of 'kindergarten curriculum' common elsewhere, preparing them to begin formal learning some time in Year 1 or even Year 2.

If, as we contend, fluency at word level is essential for successful development of literacy skills, our present system is probably hindering the government's drive to raise standards. Too many children stumble at the first fence – encountering difficulties with phonics, handwriting or both. This early failure is difficult to redress, and at present we waste much time, energy and money trying to retrieve children who, given more time to develop and suitable preparatory activities, need not encounter failure at all.

We recommend that schools need:

- greater flexibility about the point at which formal teaching of the NC begins;
- a more detailed Foundation Curriculum to prepare children for formal learning between the ages of 3 and 6 (see page 80).

Be aware of developments in ICT

Two major developments in ICT, which within ten years should be widespread in the workplace, will render typing skills redundant. These changes are likely to affect the teaching of word level skills:

- **Handheld tablet PCs**, on which the user writes with a special stylus. The handwritten text can be converted into print and word-processed as on a conventional computer.
- **Speech recognition software** with which the user talks into a microphone and words appear as print on the screen, and may be read back if desired. This technology is much improved in recent years, and the software is now relatively inexpensive.

In both these ways of 'writing', the computer's spellcheck facility can take over much of the responsibility for correct spelling. While learning to spell well remains important for most of us, children with specific spelling difficulties should soon be able to access much more immediate support. Speech recognition software is already being trialled with such pupils with some success, although it is not suitable for children under the age of 10 because of problems with voice tone. On the other hand, tablet PCs are proving highly successful in trials for all ages, and it seems very likely that, once the price falls, these will become a widespread educational tool. The implications for the importance of neat fluent handwriting are considerable.

Grammar for Literacy

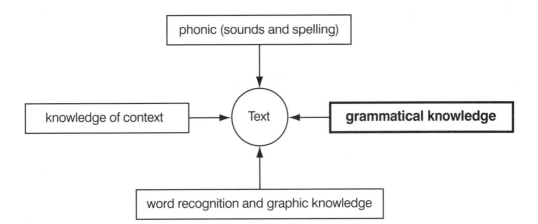

One extraordinary achievement of the National Literacy Strategy has been to place grammar teaching back at the heart of literacy. This has had some genuine benefits but also raised important issues. When the Strategy was launched, a large percentage of teachers had scant knowledge of grammar, which for many years had been out of fashion. The majority of teachers aged under about 50 knew little, unless they had studied another language. Because of this lack of knowledge and confidence, it soon became evident that teachers were reverting to teaching grammar through isolated exercises and the labelling of parts. Sadly, where the teaching of grammar was interpreted in this way, progress in writing was hindered by a culture of 'death by worksheet', exacerbated by some publishers producing photocopiable materials of dubious quality.

Consequentially, the Strategy set in place training for every Year 6 teacher in what became known as the *Grammar for Writing* initiative. This involved training, a video of teaching plus a book and CD-ROM of materials for classroom use. The training focused on:

- updating teacher's grammatical knowledge;
- presenting approaches to teaching grammar;
- strategies for relating grammar teaching to improving writing.

Unfortunately, there is a long way to go. Many schools still waste time on isolated, dull exercises that have little impact on the improvement of writing. It is still not uncommon to find exercise books full of half-finished, scrubby pieces of work, which must be disheartening for pupils. Often the bits do not relate to each other or to the text type being taught. Of course, the teacher can say *we've done this or that*: objectives are being covered, the framework is being delivered (like widgets from the back of a lorry) – but sadly, no one is learning very much! For instance, many Year 4 children can tell you that *an adjective is a word that describes a noun* but are still writing *the big shark opened its big mouth and I saw its big teeth*. They know what it is – but they can't use it!

To shift from the scatter-gun approach to having an impact on the quality of writing, the following conditions need to be met:

- sentence level objectives should be taught in relation to a relevant text type;
- sentence level knowledge should merely be the precursor to a skill – writing style.

What teachers need to know about grammar	28
Key points for teaching grammar	32
Internalising grammatical patterns	34
Where do we go next?	36

What Teachers Need to Know About Grammar (1)

Grammatical Knowledge	Written Style
Words, e.g.	
nouns	precise
verbs	powerful
adjectives	necessary
adverbs	necessary/position
pronouns	consistent
prepositions	phrases
determiners	specific
conjunctions	links

> A **conjunction** links ideas **within** a sentence.
>
> A **sentence connective** links two separate sentences (or main clauses).

Phrases, e.g.	
noun phrases	*the ginger tom from next door*
prepositional phrases	*at the end of the lane*
verb chains	*should have been*

Teachers' difficulties with grammar were exacerbated in the early days of the Strategy by inconsistencies of terminology. These have now been sorted out and the updated glossary in *Grammar for Writing* provides clear definitions. Sue's *Grammar Skeleton Books* and *OHTs* (TTS) set out the basic terminology clearly for children.

Teachers need a grasp of basic grammatical terms, in order to talk and read about language themselves. However, the terminology need not always be shared with children. The more one talks about language, the more confusing it may become. Often it's easier just to point to a word, phrase, etc., or to use a vague term like 'chunk of language'. Where terminology is introduced, it should always be with a view to using it immediately in context.

Word classes

Good writing usually hangs around nouns and verbs. An overdose of adjectives makes writing sound overwritten. Too many adverbs and you sound like a Mills and Boon novel (*he said, breathlessly*). Let's take a look at the word classes with a writerly eye:

- **Nouns** – children often use bland nouns that do not create powerful pictures in the reader's mind. Use 'precise' nouns, e.g. *Rottweiler* instead of *dog*.
- **Verbs** – children may write the sort of verb that they use in speech. A powerful verb can let the reader know how a character feels, e.g. *he sauntered up the lane*. The quickest way to improve a poor piece of writing is to 'go for the verbs'.
- **Adjectives** – these need to earn their place by telling the reader something new or unexpected, e.g. *the red letterbox* (aren't they all?) or *the rusty letter box*?
- **Adverbs** – the same applies to adverbs. Watch out for dull adverbs, as it may mean that the verb could be strengthened, e.g. *walked slowly* is nowhere near as effective as *ambled*. However, careful positioning of adverbs can improve a sentence: *Silently, he crept inside* is more powerful than *He crept inside silently*.
- **Pronouns** – pronouns must be consistent: children writing in the first person must not drift into the third; impersonal writing needs third (not second) person pronouns.
- **Prepositions** – see 'phrases' below: children often need help to choose the most appropriate preposition, e.g. *He sat down at the river – by? beside? in?*
- **Determiners** – children certainly don't need to know this term, but it helps to be aware of degrees of specificity: *the dog, a dog, some dogs, every dog...*
- **Conjunctions** – these words help children make links between their ideas. Indeed, access to a wide range of conjunctions (*because, although, until, unless, whenever,* etc.) helps them to think more clearly. Once they can manipulate conjunctions and create complex sentences they are better able to express their understanding.
  Conjunctions are a type of connective. However, there is another type of connective which makes a link between two sentences (e.g. *However, On the other hand...*). To avoid confusion, reserve the term 'connective' for this latter group.

Phrases

Two sorts of phrase can be very handy for a young writer.

- **Noun phrases** – use these to build up description, by adding in what it looks like, where it's from and even what it's doing – so, *the cat* becomes *the ginger tom from next door which was curled up in the sun...*
- **Prepositional phrases** – these are useful when writing narrative, especially as a way of varying the openings to the sentences and shifting the action. They make good paragraph starters *At the end of the lane... On the other side of town...*

It's also worth being aware of 'verb chains', which we need to express tense or condition.

What Teachers Need to Know About Grammar (2)

Grammatical Knowledge	Written Style

Clauses, e.g.

conjunction clause	links ideas

*She remained silent **because she wasn't sure what to say**.*

embedded clause	drops in more info

*The cat, **which was weary**, crept home.*

-ing and *-ed* clauses	sentence openings

***Gasping for breath**, Sam ran along the riverbank.*
***Exhausted by the day's teaching**, Emma fell into bed.*

	or drop in info

*Sam ran, **gasping for breath**, along the riverbank.*
*Emma, **exhausted by the day's teaching**, fell into bed.*

Sentences, e.g.

simple	clarity and impact
compound	ease and flow
complex	show links between ideas add extra information
questions	draw in the reader
exclamations	make the reader sit up
word order	improves impact and rhythm
commas in a list	description and pace

Literacy: what works? © Sue Palmer and Pie Corbett, Nelson Thornes, 2003

Clauses

Over the course of Key Stage 2, children should begin to use a variety of subordinate clauses with a developing degree of control. Subordinate clauses can be used at the start of a sentence, dropped into a sentence or tagged on the end. Here are a few useful ones, with suggested simplified names, so as to avoid the use of yet more complicated terminology:

- **'Conjunction clause'** (grammatical name: adverbial clause) – these clauses begin with a conjunction which shows the relationship between your ideas, e.g. *She remained silent **because she wasn't sure what to say***. Children tend to add these clauses at the end of the main clause, but you can often achieve a different rhythm or emphasis by moving them upfront: ***Because she wasn't sure what to say**, she remained silent*.
- **'Embedded clause'** (grammatical name: relative clause) – these are useful for dropping further information into a sentence, e.g. *The cat, **which was weary**, crept home*. The words introducing these clauses are a type of pronoun: *who, whom, whose, which* and *that*. Generally, *who* is used for people and *which* for animals and things (*that* can be used for either).
- **'*-ing* and *-ed* clauses'** (grammatical name: non-finite clause) – very handy for sentence openings, where you put the character's actions or state of mind foremost, e.g. ***Gasping for breath**, Sam ran along the riverbank*. However, they can also be placed after the noun, and are often less 'clunky' than a fully-fledged embedded clause: *Sam ran, **gasping for breath**, along the riverbank*.

Punctuation plays an important part in the manipulation of clauses. Generally speaking, if you put a subordinate clause at the beginning of a sentence, you need a comma to show where it finishes and the main clause begins. Embedded clauses (and *-ing* and *-ed* clauses acting in the same way) are usually separated off from the rest of the sentence with commas – but not always: *The man who came to dinner left his coat*. The best way to decide is to read the sentence aloud.

Sentences

Good writers control and vary sentences in a variety of ways, using a selection of:

- **Simple sentences** (one clause) – These can give clarity and impact. Use short ones for tension (*She screamed*.) or to state important information (*Light travels in straight lines*.).
- **Compound sentences** (two or more clauses joined by co-ordinating conjunctions – the main ones are *and, but, so, or*). These help writing to jog along and give flow. However, don't overuse them – you need a mixture of compound and complex sentences to express ideas fluently and clearly.
- **Complex sentences** (two or more clauses joined as shown above under 'Clauses'). These allow you to show relationships between ideas and to add in extra information.

You can also vary sentence types, openings and length:

- **Questions** – These enliven writing and make the reader think, e.g. *Where could she be? Are you the only teacher in the school without a laptop?*
- **Exclamations** – Keep the reader alert!
- **Varying word order** (*Silently, she crept inside*) or **opening with a subordinate clause** (*Gasping for breath*...) can improve the impact and rhythm of the sentence.
- **Lists** can hurry the reader along: *Harry was wearing a long cloak, a bright yellow hat and a pair of sneakers. He ran down the lane, leapt over the fence, and landed right on top of a rather angry-looking dwarf.*

Key Points for Teaching Grammar

Audience + purpose = organisation + style

Writer's toolkit:

Text-type	Organisation	Style
Instructions	*'how to' title*	*bossy verbs*
	Intro para	*bullet points*
	what you need	*clear, simple language*
	what to do	*commas in lists*
	conclusion	

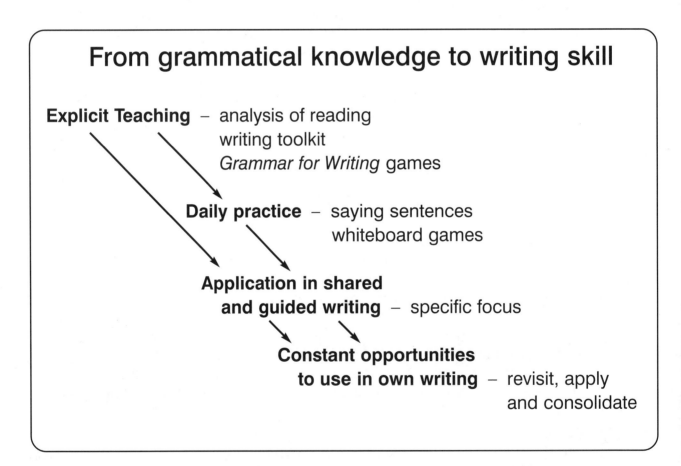

From grammatical knowledge to writing skill

Explicit Teaching – analysis of reading
writing toolkit
Grammar for Writing games

Daily practice – saying sentences
whiteboard games

**Application in shared
and guided writing** – specific focus

**Constant opportunities
to use in own writing** – revisit, apply
and consolidate

Literacy: what works? © Sue Palmer and Pie Corbett, Nelson Thornes, 2003

Grammatical skill is about using language to create different effects, through:

- selecting the right words and building phrases;
- controlling, varying and manipulating sentences;
- providing links within and between sentences;
- linking paragraphs and structuring texts;
- using accurate, automatic punctuation.

Reading like a writer

Many teachers begin their teaching of text types by focusing on 'reading as a writer: looking at texts with a writerly eye to see how they are constructed and what features are needed. During this stage the class considers the impact of different words or constructions, thinking about audience, purpose and the writer's intentions. In essence, they deconstruct examples to identify the parts. These may be listed as a writer's toolkit of organisational and language features. These toolkits can also be used as checklists after writing, or as 'marking ladders' for the child to self-evaluate and the teacher to comment on.

Manipulating language

It is tempting to gloss over the need to let children manipulate language. Many *Grammar for Writing* games are built around the notion of moving chunks of language about, underlining, pointing to, circling, using colours to identify, collecting and listing. Children need to see that we can manipulate language in a concrete fashion, to see words as objects that can be picked up and moved about to see how that influences meaning. Generating rules and principles through problem solving as well as imitating patterns are also crucial to gaining a feel for grammar. In the end, teachers should worry less about labelling parts and more about whether children use language effectively. They do not need a degree in linguistics – just a vocabulary with which to discuss writing plus the skills to use language. Of course, if we keep using terminology over the years then in the end most children begin to use it too, as they do with technical vocabulary in other curricular areas.

Turning knowledge into writing skill

One of the dangers of working to objectives is the feeling that once taught, you can move on. It is more productive to think of the sentence level work as being part of the children's repertoire as writers that needs constant revisiting. Children need:

1. Explicit teaching, to introduce an aspect of sentence work. This involves reading as a writer, problem-solving texts and constructing the writer's toolkit. *Grammar for Writing* games may be useful for helping children manipulate specific features that are new or the class may find difficult.
2. They will then need plenty of practice both 'saying sentences' and writing them – daily use of mini-whiteboards is ideal for practice at constructing, varying and linking sentences.
3. Shared writing is an important tool for showing children how to use specific features within the context of a whole text. In guided writing, strugglers should be picked up and helped, by thinking each sentence through, writing it and checking.
4. Children then need plenty of chances to use what has been taught both within literacy and other areas of the curriculum. They need to apply their learning, constantly revisiting so that their skills become a daily habit – and their learning is consolidated.
5. Once they have written, the class should evaluate their writing and marking should pick up on what was taught and whether it has been used effectively or needs refining (see Chapter 7).

Internalising Grammatical Patterns

Talking like a book

- local dialect
- saying sentences
- storytelling
- story reading
- poetry by heart
- anecdotes, 'show and tell', 'what I know', explaining, instructing, persuading, debating

Grammar for Writing games

- investigate
- manipulate
- point to it

Oral and whiteboard games, e.g.

- Mr Copycat
- Word to sentence
- Finish
- Improve
- Sentence doctor
- Innovate
- Join
- Drop in

Grammar in use – writing

- Carefully, using adverbs to start sentences...

Talking like a book

Most children manage to acquire and become proficient at their local dialect, garnered from home and school. Occasionally, they shift from a home language to a different school language. Listening to children imitating their favourite TV characters is a salutary reminder that, given a motivating purpose, they can adapt language very readily. Their local dialect will serve them well in school for 'talk for learning' – the everyday chat that is needed to think problems through, discuss learning and so forth. However, we are also keen for them to use other types of language – to adopt a narrative voice, to persuade, explain, instruct and so on. This will only happen if the children are immersed in the type of language that they need to acquire – this means that blocks of work on a text type may need to be half-a-term long. Various activities can help children internalise patterns of language and these include:

- working in pairs to orally imitate or rehearse a sentence;
- practising the sorts of sentence that we are going to need to write;
- joining in and learning stories by heart – both told and read;
- learning poetry by heart (easily done by sending a book home that has a new rhyme, playground rhyme or short poem stuck in each week);
- making sure that before children write they have always had opportunities to speak the sort of text they are studying, e.g. holding a debate before discussion writing.

Grammar for Writing games

The games in *Grammar for Writing* provide ready-made activities that can be used to help children investigate language patterns, draw out principles and manipulate chunks of language. Sue's *Big Book Grammar* (Heinemann) provides many more. It is worth remembering that often children – and adults – get worried when they feel they have to 'say what it is' but may well be able to point to the bit that is under focus. Multi-sensory games are very helpful for helping children gain control over language.

Oral and whiteboard games

Children need constant practice for writing skills to become automatic. Indeed, over-learning is no bad thing. Starting literacy sessions with quick-fire oral or whiteboard activities helps get the brain moving. These might be spelling or sentence games (or both):

- *Mr Copycat* – copy the sentence that the glove puppet says;
- *Word to sentence* – provide a word or two; they have to turn them into a sentence;
- *Finish* – provide part of a sentence to complete;
- *Improve* – provide a boring sentence to improve;
- *Sentence doctor* – provide sentence/s with an error;
- *Innovate* – innovate on given sentence structures (e.g. starting with an adverb);
- *Join* – provide two simple sentences to be joined (and some conjunctions to use);
- *Drop in* – dropping clauses into simple sentences (embedded, *-ing* or *-ed* clauses).

For more games see Pie's *Jumpstart!* (David Fulton).

Grammar in use – writing

If we are to help children improve as writers, all teachers need to develop confidence in teaching through shared writing, demonstrating to children how to plan, draft and polish their writing. This involves taking specific aspects of style and showing how it can be used to enhance writing, e.g. using an adverb to start a sentence – *Carefully, use adverbs to start sentences*. Pie's *Grammar Success* (OUP) provides materials for teaching grammatical skills to improve writing.

Where Do We Go Next?

Take the fuse out of the photocopier

It might be a good idea to dismantle the photocopier and get the old banda machine out. Not only would this appeal to those who need to sniff alcohol at breaktime, but it also means teachers would not be able to copy materials so easily. This would have the knock-on effect that one would only make a worksheet when it was really needed!

It was inevitable that teachers who lacked subject knowledge and confidence would fall back on to grammar exercises. The biggest shift we can make is to move from the loneliness of the long distance worksheet into actually teaching writing – the grammatical nuts and bolts becoming a part of that teaching. In the most effective lessons, the teaching of grammar is within the context of the reading and writing.

Exercises themselves are not necessarily an evil thing. (The very word 'exercise' sounds as if we are going to exercise something and in a minute go and use that to play a game...). Occasionally, we do need to put the spotlight on an aspect of language and an exercise may well be the way to do this. If this is the case, then the simplest way to proceed is to make sure that on the next page – and thereafter – that aspect of language becomes used in the children's writing.

We have all attended ICT courses where by the end of the day you are convinced that you now know how to use the digital camera. But if you do not go straight back and start using the information, what happens? Within a day or two, you have forgotten. If that happens to us as adults, then it is inevitable that it will happen to children. They need plenty of opportunity to use what has been taught, to apply, revisit and consolidate their learning. Ease with the terminology will come over the years through using specific terms within our discussions of reading and writing.

So, the biggest shift we can make is to be rid of isolated exercises – and to embed grammar into the teaching of writing. Think – Written Style!

Training for Years 1, 3 and 4

Much of the NLS training has provided teachers in Reception, Years 2, 5 and 6 with extra subject knowledge and materials, some of which teachers have found useful as models for generating their own ideas and sequences. However, many teachers in Years 1, 3 and 4 have not benefited from such support and are still unfamiliar with the principles of grammar and how it might become a dynamic tool for improving writing. More opportunities for these teachers would help to strengthen their teaching. This training should focus not so much on grammatical knowledge as on improving writing style, through using appropriate models, shared writing and effective marking (see Chapter 7).

Don't be over-ambitious

Teachers need to select (or write) the 'model for writing' with care. Ted Hughes' *The Iron Man* makes a fabulous read for Year 3 children. But we have to remember that Hughes was a genius and at Level 3,000! As a model it may be too hard to emulate. 'Models for writing' often need to be specifically constructed to contain features that the teacher wants to teach. The ideal would be a rich diet of reading, contributing to the class toolkit, as well as a specific 'model for writing' just above the level of the children – an edge of challenge.

Cross-curricular Literacy

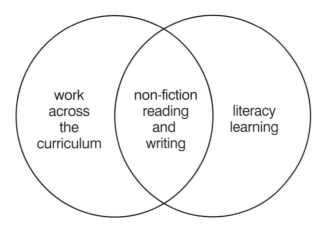

The National Literacy Strategy was introduced because of concern about the teaching of literacy skills, especially in Key Stage 2. In many schools reading and writing were seen as 'service subjects', covered incidentally during the teaching of the rest of the curriculum, and teachers' own knowledge about the skills underlying literacy was often weak. The Literacy Hour was intended to ensure at least one hour's 'ring-fenced' time per day for the specific teaching of reading and writing.

While this policy was successful in focusing attention on literacy teaching, it also had unforeseen negative consequences. Schools had already been discouraged from making cross-curricular links by QCA and Ofsted, which (during Chris Woodhead's reign of terror) insisted on compartmentalisation of the curriculum: separate lesson time for history, geography, art, etc. For many teachers, the requirement to teach literacy separately was the final nail in the coffin. They acquired sets of literacy textbooks (or worse, copymasters) and the Literacy Hour was devoted to studying text extracts and completing decontextualised exercises.

Apart from the mind-numbing boredom of such exercises, and the fact that they do not help children see the link between literacy skills and real life, they are extremely wasteful of precious time. Fortunately, Ofsted in *The Curriculum in Successful Primary Schools* (2002) and the National Primary Strategy in *Excellence and Enjoyment* (2003) have now made it clear that literacy flourishes best within a broad and balanced curriculum and that cross-curricular links encourage children's engagement in learning.

Now that teachers have got to grips with the literacy objectives in the NLS framework, it is vital that we return to **using** literacy skills as well as teaching them. Children need frequent opportunities to apply what they have learned in literacy lessons and to consolidate that learning in their day-to-day work across the curriculum.

The six non-fiction text types	38
Text organisation: skeletons	40
Language features: 'the science of it'	42
Two horses before the cart	44
Where do we go next?	46

The Six Non-fiction Text Types

Recount

retelling events in time order

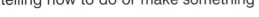

accounts of schoolwork/outings

stories from history or RE

anecdotes and personal accounts

biographical writing in any subject

Report

describing what something is (or was) like

aspects of life in a historical period

characteristics of plants/animals

descriptions of localities/geographical features

Instruction

telling how to do or make something

art, DT, PE activities

procedures in maths/ICT/science

class or school rules

Explanation

explaining how/why something happens

why historical events happened

how things work/come about in science, geography, etc.

Persuasion

arguing a case; trying to influence opinion

'publicity campaigns' (articles, posters, leaflets) in any subject

expressing viewpoints on controversial topics in any subject

Discussion

a balanced argument

stating the case on both sides of a controversy in any subject

writing objective 'essays'

The NLS introduced teachers to six generic non-fiction text types with which pupils should be familiar by the end of primary school. Each text type has its own organisational characteristics and language features, which teachers can help children identify during shared and guided reading, and use in shared, guided and independent writing. But to practise writing in a particular text type, you also need content. A series of NLS 'fliers' in 2001 showed how knowledge acquired elsewhere in the curriculum could be brought to the Literacy Hour to act as content for non-fiction writing.

Skeletons

The vehicles suggested in the fliers for carrying cross-curricular content between subject lessons and literacy teaching have become known as skeletons (illustrated opposite). These are six simple note-taking devices, each of which is particularly suited to the organisational characteristics of the text type. For instance, since recount text is chronologically organised, the chosen skeleton is a timeline; on the other hand, report text is non-chronological, and instead relies on categorisation of information, so the skeleton is a spidergram.

There are, of course, many ways to represent each text type. A recount could be represented by a storyboard, a flow chart or even a numbered list. The best planning framework for a report might be a simple labelled picture or, if the report is comparative, a grid. The six skeletons illustrated opposite are merely a starting point. However, for many children (and teachers) they have also come to act as visual icons for the six text types, helping to illustrate the underlying structure upon which the text is based.

Cross-curricular reading

When covering a particular text type therefore, the teacher looks for examples relevant to pupils' work elsewhere in the curriculum. When reading these exemplar texts, pupils can:

- establish comprehension and appreciation of the text structure by representing the facts as skeleton notes;
- study the way the author has constructed the text, noting major language features.

Cross-curricular writing

Content for pupils' writing that matches the text type can be found in any area of the curriculum. This subject matter is taught in history, geography or whatever – preferably in ways which encourage plenty of activity and opportunities for talk (see page 45) – and recorded in note form on the appropriate skeleton. It is then taken to the literacy lesson, where the teacher revisits the 'toolkit' of appropriate language features, and demonstrates composition in a shared writing lesson. Pupils then use the skeleton notes as the content for their own writing. Because the content is already there, done, dusted and appropriately organised on the skeleton, they are free to concentrate on compositional skills.

Literacy and learning

Using these teaching strategies, the teaching of non-fiction literacy skills can always be linked to cross-curricular work. To teach a particular text type, you look for suitable subject matter in the rest of the curriculum, and link your literacy work to it (perhaps rejigging medium term plans to fit). And whenever work in history, geography, science is to be recorded, pupils can use the appropriate skeleton as a quick recording device, or as the basis for written work – thus constantly reinforcing their understanding of the text type.

Text Organisation: Skeletons

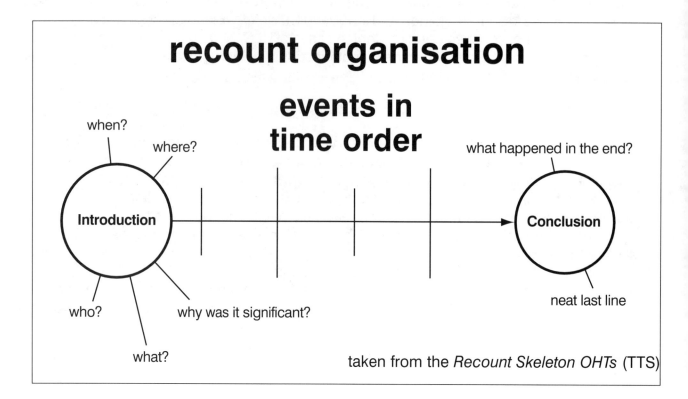

recount organisation

events in time order

when?

where?

Introduction

who?

why was it significant?

what?

what happened in the end?

Conclusion

neat last line

taken from the *Recount Skeleton OHTs* (TTS)

A report tells you what something is like. It is not in time order.

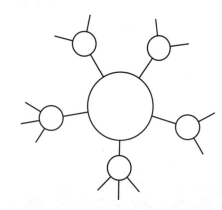

Planning reports

* **B**RAINSTORM what you know/find out.

* **O**RGANISE it into categories. (Find out more if you need to.)

* Make a **S**PIDERGRAM skeleton

  – write the topic in the middle

  – write one category on each leg.

taken from the *Key Stage 1 Skeleton Book* (TTS)

The six skeleton organisational frameworks have now been used by teachers around the country, who have been kind enough to pass on many practical suggestions.

Note-taking and converting thoughts into writing

Pupils often find skeleton notes easier than conventional note-taking. As one teacher put it, *that word* **notes** *carries a lot of baggage*, so she talks about jotting down 'memory joggers', and points out that memories can be jogged by many things (words, phrases, abbreviations, symbols, drawings). When pupils come to write from their skeletons, she simply tells them to *Make your memory joggers into sentences* and *Add any extra detail that helps make it clear*.

Text structure and paragraphing

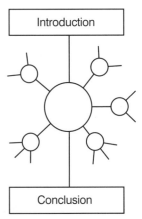

Many teachers have added to the skeleton 'icons' to show aspects of text structure more clearly. For instance, the recount usually begins with an 'orientation paragraph'. When pupils have jotted their memory-joggers along the timeline, they can consider where further natural breaks in the narrative might come, marking them with coloured lines called 'para-breaks'. The mantra when writing is then: *When you come to a para-break, miss a line*.

For the other five text types, paragraphing is generally reflected in the shape of the skeleton, although teachers continue to improve on these, as in the version of the report skeleton shown here.

Visuo-spatial learning and 'big picture thinking'

Skeleton notes can take many forms – anything from small scruffy jottings to carefully made classroom displays, illustrated with children's drawings or photos. We've also had reports of human timelines (children in line, holding cards) and recount notes pegged along a washing line.

The three-stage BOSsing system (see opposite) helps children see how disparate ideas are sorted in report text, like with like, and clustered into categories. One teacher suggested doing this initial brainstorming on to Post-it notes, which can then be physically moved around as the group decides on categories. A Key Stage 1 teacher used hoops laid out on the ground to represent the spidergram. Pupils spoke the facts and stood in the appropriate hoop (till they got too congested, when notes were thrown into the hoop instead).

Concrete activities of this kind are helpful at all stages of the primary school, not just in Key Stage 1. Kinaesthetic learners and 'big picture thinkers' benefit immensely having a visuo-spatial overview of the material, which they can then convert into the linear form required for writing (see also *Thinking Skills and Eye Q* by Caviglioli, Harris and Tindall).

Making thinking visible

Another advantage of arranging ideas on skeletons before writing is that misconceptions, missing information or irrelevance can be sorted out before the child begins to write. This Y2 explanation skeleton, for instance, illustrating reversible change, led to discussion of whether the car's cleanliness was relevant to the process, and thence to what features of the car were in fact involved.

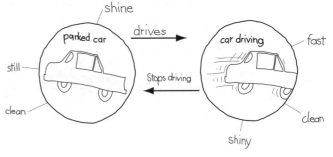

Language Features: 'the science of it'

Instruction text

* simple clear language

* imperative verbs
  (except 'third person instructions')

* second person
  (except 'third person instructions')

* necessary detail only

* numbers and/or
  time connectives

Mix the flour ...

Press button A ...

Cut along the line ...

Always use the correct equipment

Feed and exercise your dog ...

adapted from the *Instruction Skeleton OHTs* (TTS)

Explanation text

* present tense
  (except historical explanations)

* causal language

* sequential connectives

* impersonal language
  e.g. use of the passive

* technical vocabulary

because

If...then...

The reason that ...

when   so

This results in...

This causes...

therefore

adapted from the *Explanation Skeleton OHTs* (TTS)

The six text types have provided teachers with a vehicle for teaching non-fiction writing skills. One told how a Year 5 boy who previously struggled with writing came up after her first lesson on recount writing and said: *That's it, miss. Teach me the science of it!*

A writer's toolkit

We can now help children recognise not only the typical organisation of particular types of writing, but also the major language features associated with it. These can be spotted and collected during shared reading to form a 'writer's toolkit'. The teacher can then demonstrate how to use specific aspects of the toolkit in shared writing, before pupils try writing for themselves. In order to talk about texts in shared reading and writing, teacher and pupils need shared access to some basic grammatical vocabulary (see Chapter 3).

Audience and purpose

The type of language used in any text relates closely to the audience and purpose for which it is designed. Even Key Stage 1 children can recognise, when introduced to the writing of instruction text, that 'simple, clear language' is essential. The writer must also decide which details the reader needs and which are redundant (e.g. in a recipe *milk* is too vague, but *1 litre of smooth white creamy milk* is overdoing it). This is in direct contrast to story-writing, where children are urged to embellish writing with descriptive words and plenty of detail.

However, although broad guidelines for writing a particular type of text are useful, they must not turn into holy writ. For instance, it is now widely claimed that instruction text uses imperative verbs but, as anyone who has written instructions for a game knows, you sometimes have to write in the third person instead (e.g. *Player A takes three cards...*).

Cohesive devices

Among the most important language features of a particular text type are those which contribute to cohesion – the connectives and other 'signposts' helping to guide the reader through the text, e.g.:

- instruction text involves a sequence of steps, so the layout of the piece should reflect these steps, by means of numbers or time connectives (e.g. *next*, *now*, *finally*);
- explanations also usually rely on sequence for clarity, so similar connectives (e.g. *first*, *then*, *eventually*) can highlight the stages in the process.

This type of vocabulary is unfamiliar for many children, as in spoken language situations the all-purpose sequential connective is *and then*. It is therefore helpful to make a particular point of looking for cohesive devices (conjunctions, sentence connectives, specific sentence 'frames') for the writer's toolkit, and to practise using this 'signpost language' orally before writing, and/or during supported writing.

Playing with language

Causal language – which features heavily in explanations, persuasion and discussion – is a case in point. In speech, cause and effect is usually expressed with the conjunctions *because*, *when* or *so*. Written explanations are often more complex, and it may take two or more sentences to ensure that a particular cause and effect is clearly explained. Thus constructions like *This results in...* and *The reason that... is...* are common. Sometimes these constructions require a change in the verb form. It therefore helps to give children time to familiarise themselves with causal language **orally**. You could invite them in pairs to try using the 'causal language frames' in the speech bubble opposite to express a particular cause (e.g. *The window is open*) and effect (e.g. *It is cold*) in a variety of ways.

Two Horses Before the Cart

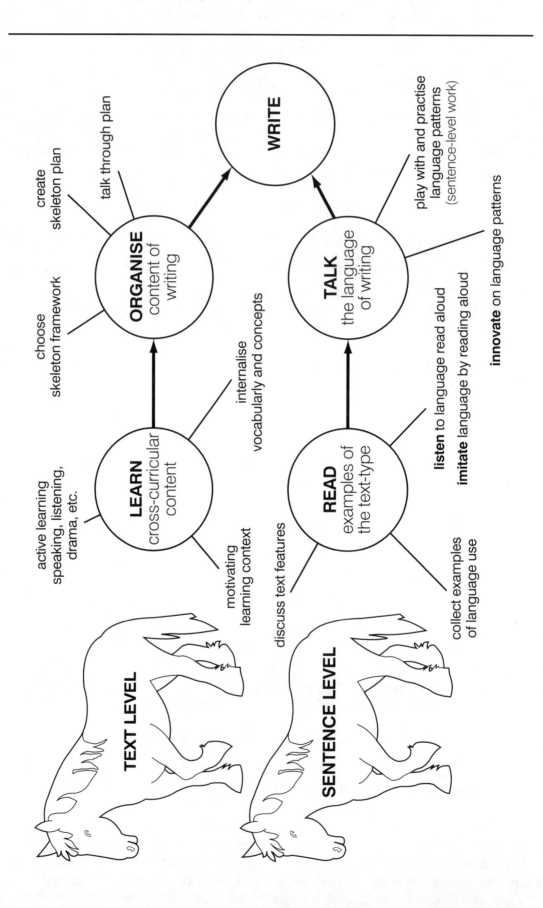

WRITE

ORGANISE content of writing

create skeleton plan

talk through plan

choose skeleton framework

internalise vocabulary and concepts

LEARN cross-curricular content

active learning speaking, listening, drama, etc.

motivating learning context

TALK the language of writing

play with and practise language patterns (sentence-level work)

innovate on language patterns

listen to language read aloud

imitate language by reading aloud

READ examples of the text-type

discuss text features

collect examples of language use

TEXT LEVEL

SENTENCE LEVEL

Throughout this chapter, we have referred to the importance of talk in cross-curricular learning. Indeed, the more we learn about the interface between learning, language and literacy, the more significant opportunities for talk become. This has led to the development of Sue's 'two horses model', so named because of all the teachers who've said *All this emphasis on writing is putting the cart before the horse*. Before they can write, children need meaningful experiences to write about, and opportunities to talk them through.

In Chapter 6 on 'Speaking, listening and literacy' we distinguish between spoken and written language patterns, and this distinction underlies the model:

- **the text level horse** is about opportunities to practise vocabulary relevant to the subject matter, get to grips with concepts and organise thinking through spoken language activities;
- **the sentence level horse** involves oral practice of written language patterns, like the 'causal language practice' described on page 43.

There are many suggestions for activities of both kinds in Chapter 6, and we firmly believe that – as well as providing exciting and motivating learning experiences – talk-based activities provide the conceptual and linguistic foundations on which true literacy can be built.

Because of their different underlying structures, the six text types lend themselves to different types of spoken language work, e.g.:

Recount

Drama and role-play, in which groups act out sequences from the recount for the class;
Teacher in role, in which the teacher participates and guides class role-play;
Puppet plays devised by groups of pupils to illustrate all or part of the story;
Freeze-framing, in which groups provide living tableaux of certain events;
Retelling all or sections of the story either to the class or a partner.

Report

Show and Tell, talking about objects/pictures related to the topic;
Small-group discussion of open-ended questions (e.g. compare/contrast – see page 65);
TV or radio documentaries including commentary, interviews, mini-dramatisations;
Hot-seating in which pupils in role answer questions from the class on aspects of their 'life';
Brains Trust – a panel answers questions from the class on a subject they have researched;
Art or craft work – making models, artefacts, pictures, collages, etc. related to the subject.

Instructions

Do it yourself – actually do or make the thing you're going to write about;
TV demonstration, *à la* Delia Smith or *Blue Peter,* demonstrating the process;
Mime with commentary, like a public service broadcast (can also be done with puppets).

Explanation

Physical theatre, turning the process into **imaginative role-play**, e.g. transform pupils into particles, planets, blood corpuscles, animals in a food chain, parts of a plant...
Illustrated talks, using a flowchart skeleton as a focus for a spoken presentation
Interviews with a child assuming 'the mantle of the expert'.

Persuasion and discussion

Drama activities – role-play, hot-seating, 'broadcasts' as above;
Small group discussion of open-ended questions in which the group must reach a consensus (e.g. organising statements in order of importance);
Debates: formal debates, balloon debates, debates with pupils in role;
Question time, modelled on the Radio 4 programme, perhaps with pupils in role.

Where Do We Go Next?

Get out of the straitjacket, but not back into the woolly pully

Recent publications from the Primary Strategy and Ofsted have urged schools to 'loosen up' and make cross-curricular links, but many teachers are finding it difficult to get out of the straitjacket imposed over the last decade. Having been expected for so long to think in terms of discrete subject coverage with a ring-fenced hour a day for literacy, they will need encouragement to break this 'compartmentalised' mindset.

However, it's just as important that the 'loosen up' message is not misinterpreted as meaning a return to the sloppy, haphazard cross-curricular approach of earlier years.

Government agencies and local advisory services must convey clearly that what is required is **balance**:

- literacy objectives *and* cross-curricular teaching;
- structure *and* freedom;
- excellence *and* enjoyment.

In such a balanced ethos, teachers should feel confident about embedding their teaching of non-fiction reading and writing within exciting, motivating cross-curricular work (involving not only 'academic' subjects, but art, music, drama and lots of opportunities for talk). They should also feel confident to look for links between what's planned for their classes (e.g. annual celebrations, seasonal activities, class outings) and their literacy teaching objectives, and to move around elements of the literacy framework to fit in with these.

Be aware of the interface between learning, language and literacy

Cross-curricular literacy teaching provides opportunities for developing all pupils' capacity for thinking and learning.

Thinking involves using both sides of the brain: the holistic, visuo-spatial right hemisphere, and the analytic, linear and highly linguistic left hemisphere. The model of teaching proposed in this chapter involves:

- the 'big picture' communication of structures of thought and relationships through diagrams (right brain);
- developing pupils' command of spoken and written language to communicate this understanding verbally (left brain). Learning to write is particularly useful in helping pupils learn to control and manipulate language.

When teaching a topic in any area of the curriculum, teachers could consider:

- What sort of thought is required here and which text-type does it relate to? How can we represent it in the visuo-spatial dimension (pictorially and diagrammatically)?
- When teaching the content, how can I ensure pupils are actively involved, and have opportunities for 'talk for learning', so they become familiar with the vocabulary and concepts concerned?
- What language features are characteristic of the subject-matter and the text-type?
- How can I familiarise pupils with these (through reading, discussion, and language play), thus ensuring opportunities for 'talk for writing'?

Creativity and Literacy

One of the charges levelled most consistently at the NLS is that it has nothing to do with creativity. Many teachers found it difficult to see how they could approach the objectives in a creative manner. Often over the last few years, we have heard teachers say, *the Literacy Hour is boring*. On the other hand, we have also been privileged to see many teachers who have managed to plan imaginative sequences of work and who regularly produce high quality, creative writing and drama.

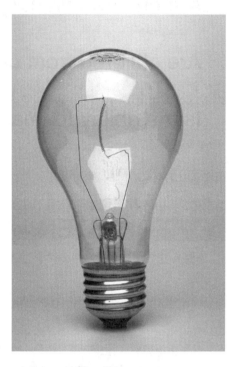

The government's response to concerns over a lack of enjoyment and dulling of the spirit is outlined in *Excellence and Enjoyment*. Here they make their position quite clear:

We want all schools to ... be creative and innovative in how they teach...

Sadly, the climate of testing and 'fear of Ofsted' have too often hindered teachers in their desire to teach creatively. Year 6 has for many become dominated by driving towards attaining Level 4, often at the expense of developing creative approaches. Heads are down, dealing with subordinate clauses and out of the window goes any idea of spending time painting haiku posters! Furthermore, Ofsted has made teachers feel that they have to teach a Literacy Hour as it is 'what they'll want to see'. Fear all too often now drives how we teach.

Ironically, creative teaching and doing well in the SATs are not mutually exclusive. If children have been writing a rich vein of poetry, narrative and non-fiction creatively then it would be surprising if they had not made good progress. However, the art of teaching creatively is not easy. You need strong subject knowledge and some creative flair yourself.

We must also remember that literacy liberates creativity. Many children who might well have something of interest to say are hindered because they cannot spell, write neatly or fluently and they have little control over sentences. Children who struggle with writing generally lack basic skills. Those who write creatively have found ways to focus their thinking on the flow of composition. When spelling and sentence control is automatic, there is enough cognitive space for the brain to create. As Michael Barber said, when someone asked him about 'fun': *Where is the fun in not being able to read?* Without fundamental basic skills, creativity is trapped and cannot flourish.

Creativity is a frame of mind and the right conditions are needed:

- the basic skills with which to read and write;
- a teacher who establishes a creative climate;
- balance between a structured approach and the freedom to experiment.

Imagination and the language of stories 48
Creative reading and responding   52
Creative writing and talking   54
Where do we go next?   56

Imagination and the Language of Stories 1

Are children unimaginative?

Are children from certain estates less imaginative?

Is the ability to imagine the province of the wealthy?

LISTEN – IMITATE – INNOVATE – INVENT

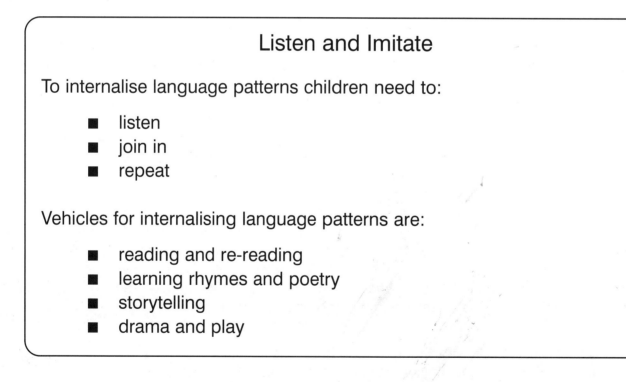

Listen and Imitate

To internalise language patterns children need to:

- listen
- join in
- repeat

Vehicles for internalising language patterns are:

- reading and re-reading
- learning rhymes and poetry
- storytelling
- drama and play

My children are not imaginative

It is a tempting thought and many teachers are drawn into believing that the children they teach are inherently dull – or blaming the estate they live on and their home background. We would always want to challenge the notion that children are not imaginative, creative beings with great potential. After all, if you follow these children into the playground, they seem to be up to all sorts – inventing games, dashing about, gossiping in corners, swapping jokes, chanting rhymes... Not exactly a dull group!

When we look at children's ability to write, the issue is not to do with a lack of imagination. It is more to do with a lack of the building blocks with which to be imaginative. As teachers, we could easily invent a fairy tale because inside our minds is a vast storehouse from our reading – we have kings, queens, old beggars (the characters), a lake, forest, a lonely tower (the settings). And we all know what will happen as the prince climbs the stone steps and peers into the top room of that tower – there will be a princess, spinning straw into gold (the run of events). I'll leave what happens next to your imagination...

You see, we can imagine and invent narrative because we can draw upon that storehouse from our own reading. So, the issue is not to do with a lack of imagination but more to do with lacking what is needed in order to imagine. Many children have read so little that they do not possess such building blocks. They have lived on a diet of TV, which serves up ready-made pictures without engaging the imagination or familiarising them with the patterns of narrative. Look at the best writers in any class – they are always children who have read voraciously. They can write because they can draw upon what they know well.

If this is the case then we need to ensure that children have plenty of opportunities to read and also to hear narrative and poetic patterns. Gordon Well's research, reported in *The Meaning Makers*, suggested to us that children need:

- in reception and Year 1, to be read to 5 or 6 times a day;
- at all stages, many opportunities to dramatise and play at stories;
- a weekly programme of learning rhymes and short poems;
- daily storytelling across both Key Stages.

Imitation

This involves children listening, joining in and getting to know stories and poems well. Poems can be stuck into a poetry journal that is sent home each week. Initially these would be nursery rhymes, later on an anthology might be used. Parents and carers could be expected to chant rhymes and learn poems with the child.

When reading stories to children in Key Stage 1 the teacher should identify key favourites, to be read on many occasions. Children should be increasingly encouraged to join in until they know the whole book. The teacher gradually withdraws from saying the words so that the children internalise the patterns for themselves. This actually replicates a stage that all children who have been read to at home pass through – at about 3 years old these children find a favourite that they get to know so well that they know every word (and Lord help you if you miss a word out!). Use storytelling in a similar manner so that children come to learn whole stories – over two or three weeks (see Appendix 2).

Acting stories out, playing at narrative in the role-play area and dramatising novels are all further opportunities to help children to internalise story structures and sentence patterns.

Imagination and the Language of Stories 2

INNOVATE

Adapt story structures and sentence patterns:

Substitution – same frame, different details

Addition – add more detail

Alteration – significant changes (characters? setting?)

Recycling – resetting a basic story pattern

Change viewpoint – another character's perspective.

INVENT – your own patterns

She is like a golden star,
Slinking into the night.
She is like a flower of light.
She is like a silent pair of lips,
Saying something unknown.
She is like a brilliant spurt of love.
She is like an ungrateful silence.

Matthew, 7 years

Internalising patterns and building blocks with which to imagine.

Without strong patterns to manipulate, it is hard to imagine.

Innovation

Once children know a story or poem really well – and don't be afraid of over-learning (the weaker their composition, the stronger the patterns will need to be) – then you can move on to innovation. This involves taking what is already known well and adapting it. The known tale becomes like a massive structure which the children can use to create something different. Invention is really a form of play – it reminds us of singing Christmas carols with alternative words! There are different ways in which a story might be adapted. These seem to follow a hierarchy starting with substitution, which is suitable for very young children or less confident writers:

- **Substitution** – making simple changes such as names, places, objects. This could mean retelling the tale of three little puppies rather than pigs. Substitution starts at word level.
- **Addition** – this means maintaining the same basic story but adding in extra sentences – extra description, events, characters.
- **Alteration** – taking the basic structure but altering key aspects, e.g. setting (*Snow White in New York*), making a bad character good (*Voldemort acts kindly!*).
- **Recycling** – involves taking the underlying pattern and completely resetting it. *The Minpins* might be rewritten about a child who is warned not to go somewhere because it is dangerous, but ignores the warning!
- **Change viewpoint** – this could involve rewriting the tale from another character's view. Or it might mean writing a news report about an incident, interviewing a character for a TV programme, writing a diary entry or letter from a main character.

Invention

Schools need a strong programme of narrative, poetry and drama, involving:

- getting to know poems and rhymes;
- getting to know picture books, short stories and novels;
- building up a collection of stories though storytelling.

Such activities provide a considerable bank on which children can draw to create their own narratives and poems. They need to build up a store of characters, settings, events and fundamental plots that can be used for their own ends – invention!

Poetry frames

More could also be made of simple poetry frames for writing, using a repeating phrase. This provides strong support for children to experiment with language techniques such as: choosing 'good' words, surprising combinations, alliteration, onomatopoeia, similes (*like* and *as*) and metaphor (especially personification). Many ideas and examples are given in Pie's book *Catapults and Kingfishers* (OUP).

The poem *She Is* allowed Matthew to focus upon selecting language with care, making sure that each word earned its place. He was also able to experiment with creating new and unusual combinations. It is this sort of serious game that helps children write in sentences, develop a sense of how to use language creatively, as well as strengthening the imagination, stretching the possibilities. It is worth noting that his teacher used proactive marking (see pages 72-74). For instance, if he had written *she is like a star going into the night* she would have prompted him to use well-chosen adjectives and a more powerful verb. It is both the stimulus that excites flair and the discipline of having to think carefully and excitingly, that leads into creativity – the tension between the need to think hard and the freedom to take risks.

Creative Reading and Responding

Little Red Riding Hood

- Tell me – What do you like? What don't you like? What puzzles you? Did you notice any patterns?
- Draw a story map, storyboard, timeline of key incidents.
- Compose the wolf's statement to the police.
- Write Red Riding Hood's diary.
- Write a letter from the woodcutter to his Mum.
- Hot seat the wolf.
- Make a leaflet: 5 ways to distract a wolf!
- Write instructions for an ideal Grandma.
- Interview Grandma – her ambitions and future role in a film!
- Put the wolf on trial.
- Booktalk...

The Highwayman

- Tell me – likes, dislikes, puzzles and patterns.
- Swap your first responses.
- Draw a storyboard, cartoon strip, timeline of events.
- Gossip with a neighbour about what has happened.
- Make a TV news bulletin – with outside broadcast unit, interviewing soldiers.
- Hot seat Tim, the ostler.
- Role-play a phone call from the distraught Inn Keeper to friend.
- Rewrite the story as a narrative.
- Write Tim's letter to a Lonely Hearts column (and a reply).
- Booktalk...

Literacy: what works? © Sue Palmer and Pie Corbett, Nelson Thornes, 2003

Encouraging response to reading

Children need to be taught how to read in a direct manner. But they also need to be helped to respond creatively to their reading – to visualise, to 'feel' for those who suffer so they step into someone else's shoes, to understand motives, to predict, deduce and infer from what has happened, to speculate, raise questions... and so on. This may mean coming at narrative from different directions, to help children peel away layers of meaning. The activities on the opposite page help to bring texts alive – looking at what has happened from different viewpoints. But there is more to it than trotting out '35 things to do with a book'! Discussion is central to helping children develop a critical faculty and deepen their appreciation. A good book demands to be savoured and talked about.

Aidan Chambers' framework for such fruitful discussion is encompassed in his wonderful book *Tell Me: Children Reading and Talk* (Thimble Press). Guided reading at its best should help children use their inborn ability to speculate, discriminate, compare, draw conclusions, hint at meanings, develop ideas, infer and so forth. He calls this 'Booktalk'. It is this that helps children to become responsive, critical readers. Booktalk does not involve firing comprehension questions (to which the teacher knows the answer) like the Spanish Inquisition. It involves asking questions that encourage children to collectively deepen their reading, offer tentative ideas, pursue possibilities and build meaning through responsive discussion.

Reading strengthens imagination

Not even a Secretary of State for Education would suggest that the imagination is not important. Ted Hughes said that:

> The word 'imagination' denotes not much more than the faculty of creating a picture of something in our heads and holding it there while we think about it. Since this is the basis of nearly everything we do, clearly it's very important that our imagination should be strong rather than weak.

Without imagination Einstein would not have made his leap into the dark: *Imagination is more important than knowledge*, he maintained. Good books feed the imagination.

We all need stories that cast spells. As we read, or listen, we have to weave the tale into our own secondary world. As we dream the tale, we can only envisage and relate to it through our own experience. This is why *Badger's Parting Gifts* can reduce even Ofsted inspectors to tears – it is not because they feel sorry for the badger, but because the tale helps them revisit their own grief. Of course, narrative is not only about revisiting our experience, but also about extending the possibilities. It takes us into new experiences, broadening our inner world. Indeed, our capacity to imagine stretches endlessly on, way beyond the total sum of what we will experience in our lives.

Readers may need help to imagine – to see pictures (still or moving) – and this can be developed through drama, painting, dressing up, playing stories, reading without seeing the pictures. Indeed, small children are often quite happy playing 'What if...'. This is the realm of imagination – *what if we found a chocolate tree?* Everyone laughs and makes a yummy noise. Strengthening the world of imagination – to see images and reshape them – gives us the ability to form concepts and handle symbols. Of course, the quality of the stories and poems have to be good – because that affects our involvement. Give them strong stuff – not only reading scheme material that inevitably is more to do with practising skills! Good books should have emotional appeal and the power to satisfy the imagination. It is the difference between *The Castle of Adventure* (good read) and *The Northern Lights* (good book). The world created in *The Northern Lights* is one that will remain powerfully in the imagination and adds to our inner world. It is a book that demands to be returned to.

Creative Writing and Talking

- recreating and preserving experience
- playing with words, ideas and patterns

Creating the Spark

1. Kinaesthetic, e.g.
   - Drama – role-play, hot seating, improvisation, interviews, TV crews, debates, trials, acting stories out, role-play areas...
   - Location writing
   - Trips

2. Oral/Auditory, e.g.
   - Music
   - Tapes of sounds, story starts, news items, gossip...
   - Story making
   - Storytelling and poetry performances

3. Visual, e.g.
   - Planning with story picture maps, storyboards, mountains...
   - First hand experience and observation
   - Paintings and sculptures
   - Video

4. Cognitive, e.g.
   - Scraps – memory with anecdote
   - Playing with words and sentences

SET THE RIGHT CONDITIONS FOR CREATIVITY

Literacy: what works? © Sue Palmer and Pie Corbett, Nelson Thornes, 2003

What doesn't stimulate creativity?

Where children's writing is poor and progress slow there are usually a number of issues:

- isolated grammar exercises rather than sequences (see page 33);
- work not planned in a block (see page 71);
- dull activities and writing tasks;
- little or no shared writing – and where teachers do not use shared writing, then they are not teaching writing.

Whether writing contains flair and creativity depends on many things. As we have said – children need to be reasonably proficient at handwriting, spelling and basic sentence control in order to free cognitive space so that the mind can concentrate on composition. A massive inner store of language patterns to draw upon is also essential. But there is more than that – the actual quality of the task matters. A good example is the 2003 Writing SAT inflicted on all Year 6s. Whoever imagined that two children in a queue would stimulate anything of interest must have seriously lost the plot. The *TES* asked Michael Morpurgo to sit the SAT which he found very dull. And his writing was not his finest!

What does create the spark?

Creative writing is about recreating and preserving experience as well as playing with words, ideas and patterns. There are many ways to create a spark. Acting out a story can prompt a more powerful tale as the children have 'lived' through the experience. Taking children to different locations leads to capturing what settings are really like – and a great opportunity for noticing detail to make their narratives seem real.

Many writers use music to create a 'writing mood'. Tapes of sounds gathered in a setting can stimulate thinking – where are we? What is happening? Word games, playing with words, sentences and ideas can promote surprising results – such as poems that boast or lie (*My dog was the first dog on Mars. He can eat seven Weetabix and then ask for more...*) Many children learned to love reading through end of the day storytime. We need the equivalent for writing – just the joy of making up stories with the teacher scribing or doing it orally. Listening to stories being told and poetry performed are both key ways to excite the imagination. Of course, our memories hold a vast store of possibilities for writing. We know best about what has happened to us – much of this can be taken and used in narrative or be a source for poetry. The American writer Betsy Byars calls these 'scraps' and she uses them all the time. Anne Fine says, *You learn to recognise what sort of thing can make a story... you find yourself thinking, 'I can use that'*. Knowing basic patterns for narrative can aid planning and release creativity. See Pie's *How to Teach Fiction Writing at Key Stage 2* and *How to Teach Story Writing at Key Stage 1* (David Fulton).

Children write best about what they know and what matters to them. First-hand experiences and careful observation are essential to producing quality writing. This means lighting the candle, looking at leaf skeletons, studying paintings or sculptures, drawing bicycles, cutting up vegetables and sketching them, collecting teasels... Brainstorming words and images makes a solid bridge from the abstract experience into preserving that in words. Hopkins looked at raindrops: *mealy clouds with a not brilliant moon/Blunt buds of the ash. Pencil buds of the beech. Lobes of the trees. Cups of the eyeball...* When Sally looked at a leaf skeleton under a magnifying glass, she wrote: *Like tissue, laces neatly threaded, slim veins crisscross, a crisp manuscript...*

Finally, more could be made of video material. With the increasing introduction of interactive whiteboards, it will be possible to show images to stimulate writing. Simple activities like showing a clip of two characters talking with the sound turned down acts as an intriguing way into writing dialogue.

Where Do We Go Next?

Help children internalise language

We need to strengthen the roots upon which children draw for their writing. This means a stronger pattern in Key Stage 1 of internalising language. In Key Stage 2, develop the imagination through storytime and Booktalk, built around a rich programme of quality literature, resourced with sets of books, video material, information from websites, etc.

Bring back the Writing Workshop

It's time for a return to Writing Workshops. But now they should have clear objectives and capitalise on all that we have learned about language and teaching over the last five years. Including:

1. Make writing exciting.
Ditch the dull and plan more stimulating writing tasks, e.g. if you are tackling settings then a visit to a deserted house could provide detailed notes. Work on characterisation should include role-play. Poetry needs to start from word games or observation. Taking prints of the bark from a tree can lead into writing about what can be seen in the bark... *like an elephant's skin, wrinkled as a walnut, grooved like a mountain range...* (Jolie, 6 years).

2. Establish a writing mood
Put more effort into establishing a 'writing mood', with children working as writers. Michael Morpurgo says, *I do most of my writing in bed – well, on the bed really.* Some writers need music, others cannot begin without coffee! In school, the teacher sets the mood. For writing to have a hope of containing that elusive, creative spark – it should be quiet, no one should spoil the atmosphere by mucking about, everyone should take it seriously – and the teacher uses her voice, movements and eyes to draw the children into the spell. *I have got to write in silence or my characters and world just become ink on a page and I don't find magic in them* (Jolie, 11 years). Anthony, 11 years, expresses the views of many: *I need quiet to write best, but sometimes conversation and music around me gives me ideas. I can write nearly anywhere if the particular place gives me the right feeling.*

3. Teach children how to prepare for writing
Good planning frees the brain from thinking about what to say next so that the writer can concentrate on composition. Help pupils to generate ideas and capture them – through brainstorming, ideas webs, mind maps, memory quests, sharing anecdotes, daydreaming aloud, visualising and, of course, planning. Too many children set out with nothing to say!

4. Use shared writing
Model the writing process, to demonstrate the need to concentrate and write fluently to gain a flow, how to rehearse sentences (muttering them as you write) – and reread. For creative sessions, the following should become standard procedures:

- Start sessions with whiteboard games to generate creative thinking.
- Use interesting, dynamic starting points.
- Do lots of shared writing – never just let them write.
- Help pupils to 'trap' and develop ideas through planning/drafting techniques.
- Establish a positive writing mood.
- Regular polishing (see page 75) and publishing of children's writing.

Establish creative training

Finally, teachers need inservice opportunities to write and read creatively themselves, topping up their own creative bank, building confidence and subject knowledge.

Speaking, Listening and Literacy

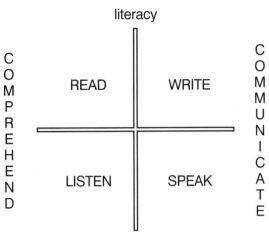

There can be no doubt that oracy and literacy are intricately interlinked – indeed oracy is the bedrock upon which literacy is built. The omission of speaking and listening from the original framework of objectives of the National Literacy Strategy was a serious mistake, which recent initiatives have tried to rectify. The revised QCA guidelines on speaking and listening provide helpful pointers for linking oracy to established literacy objectives. We would argue further that:

- speaking and listening is so important that it should be integrated into every lesson, throughout the curriculum;
- in literacy teaching account should be taken of the different types of language required for written (or 'literate') English.

In this chapter we clarify the difference between 'talk for learning' (the 'natural' use of speech to engage with ideas and communicate them in context-based speech) and 'talk for writing' (the more complex patterns of written language which, given appropriate learning experiences, can also feed into children's speech). It is through 'talk for writing' that children gain increasing control over language, and learn to adapt it for different purposes and in different circumstances.

Problems in teaching speaking and listening	58
Ten ways to help children learn to listen	60
Spoken and written language patterns	62
Talk for learning	64
Talk for writing	66
Where do we go next?	68

Problems in Teaching Speaking and Listening

1. Not valued by parents, pupils or the Powers that be.

   'low priority' 'low status'
   'Can't justify the time'

2. Children's poor concentration and communication skills. Lack of experience outside school; lack of imaginative play.

3. Hard to teach – how do you actually *teach* children to speak and listen?

4. Difficulties with classroom organisation:
   noise   space   class control   personnel

5. Ephemeral – difficult to assess, how do you produce evidence?

6. **TIME !**

I feel guilty if I give time to talk, and guilty if I don't.
Primary teacher

In the training of young children, it is sometimes necessary to waste time in order to save it.
Jean-Jacques Rousseau

This list was compiled from the most frequent responses of many hundreds of teachers to the question *What are the main problems in teaching speaking and listening?*.

1. This was by far the most frequently mentioned problem. Teachers repeatedly said they felt guilty about spending time on oral activities – even though they knew it was important – because of the need to 'have something to show' at the end of the lesson. They felt written outcomes were valued more by promoted staff, advisers and Ofsted, while children and parents believed oral work was merely 'messing about'. Clearly, if speaking and listening are to take their rightful place as an integral part of literacy learning, we need a concerted effort to change attitudes and increase the profile of oracy, both within the profession and in society as a whole. Schools could take the initiative in introducing guidelines for teachers, and by covering the issue in school prospectuses and at parents' meetings.

2. Sadly, when teachers did actually introduce spoken language activities into their teaching, many were disappointed by children's responses. They point out that in many families nowadays there is little time for talk – parents work long hours, the television is constantly on, mealtime conversation died with the TV dinner. Children are allowed to play out less than in the past, and at home commercially-produced games, especially computerised ones, have taken the place of imagination. If this is the case with your class, then teaching speaking and listening is even more important. It's also vital that teachers should feel able to devote **time** to the enterprise. Children who are not used to talk will need time to feel their way into discussion, to start by saying something 'silly' and then building on it.

3. The revised QCA guidelines on speaking and listening are helpful. But oracy is so central to learning that it should be integrated into every lesson, throughout the curriculum. The rest of this chapter provides pointers for doing this.

4. Organising thirty or so little souls (and bodies) in a confined space is always a problem, and a major part of teachers' professionalism is finding ways of solving it. One useful suggestion from the NLS which requires little organisation is the use of **talking partners**. At stages during a lesson you tell pupils to *Turn to your partner. You have three minutes to discuss*... Selected pairs can then report back on their deliberations to the class. Like all speaking and listening activities, however, this technique needs preliminary training:

   ■ Train children how to do it during Circle Time or guided writing time.
   ■ In the early stages, model each activity with a classroom assistant or able child.
   ■ Make sure children are suitably paired (and know where to sit before the lesson begins) and ring the changes frequently.
   ■ Make posters that you can point to as reminders of routines.
   ■ Experience of paired talk can prepare pupils for other activities, including group discussion.

5. Outcome (and evidence) will be in terms of improved understanding or better written work, but it is also fun – and educative for pupils – sometimes to video or audio-tape oracy activities. Occasional assessment of individual children's performance is best undertaken by an additional adult in the classroom (QCA provide assessment sheets – see above).

6. Time is the perennial problem and there'll never be an answer. Integration of oracy into cross-curricular work should help to some extent, but in the end teachers just have to be brave and acknowledge that time developing children's powers of speech is time well-spent.

Ten Ways to Help Your Pupils Learn to Listen

1. Teach rules for listening.

2. Practise regularly in Circle Time.

3. Read aloud to children.

4. Do lots of musical activities.

5. Develop auditory memory.

6. Develop imaging skills.

7. Use tapes, CDs and internet audio.

8. Use oral assessment methods.

9. Use visual channels for some information.

10. Introduce structured oral work in Early Years.

A good listener:
- looks at the speaker
- tries to keep still
- concentrates on what the speaker is saying
- thinks about what the speaker says
- asks questions if it is not clear
- values what the speaker has to say
- tries to remember what the speaker has said.

Literacy: what works? © Sue Palmer and Pie Corbett, Nelson Thornes, 2003

1. Cultural and environmental changes, especially the availability of all-day TV and video, have led to a deterioration in listening skills. Many children therefore need help in understanding what listening actually involves. Make a poster listing the main rules and teach them explicitly (see base of opposite page).

2. Circle Time automatically involves the development and deployment of good listening skills. Lucky Duck Publishing produce many useful materials, all tried and tested in classrooms. Strategies introduced in Circle Time can then be used across the curriculum.

3. From a literacy point of view, reading to children is probably the single most important thing you can do: it motivates children to read, exposes them to examples of well-written language, and hones their listening skills, all at the same time. For young children it helps if they have something specific to listen for, especially a refrain with which they can join in. They can also internalise written language patterns by gradually joining in with the whole text. But children should be read to at all ages, throughout the primary school.

4–5. Music is fundamental to literacy, since it helps train the brain to patterns and the ear to qualities of sound. If you lack confidence in music, try *The Music Makers Approach* (NASEN) for Early Years, *Music in Action With Big Books* (Lovely Music) for Key Stage 1, and A and C Black's song books with tapes or CDs for the whole primary range. Songs are particularly useful, because the melody helps children memorise words, and memorisation aids the development of auditory memory – essential for reading. Network Educational Press has published a science course using song for KS2 called *That's Science*. Opportunities for prepared reading aloud and learning poems and other fragments by heart are also extremely important for auditory memory training.

6. Today's children, spoon-fed other people's images on TV, often find it difficult to activate their own imaginations. Children need opportunities to 'make the picture in their heads' while listening to a poem or verbal narrative. The CD *Guided Imagery for Circle Time* (Lucky Duck Publishing) is a PSE resource for KS2 which helps develop children's capacity to imagine.

7. Using tapes and CDs brings other voices into the classroom, providing a professionally-made listening experience. The BBC produce a wide range of taped material at very reasonable prices, and the 'oral history' section of the BBC website has a wealth of audio-material on many topics. Try also Sound Learning for KS2 history resources on tape and CD.

8. Dictation is a method of assessing phonics, spelling and handwriting while allowing children to focus purely on transcriptional skills – hearing the words and transforming them into symbols on the page – without the added distraction of thinking up what to say and how to say it. Maths can also be assessed orally – see Collins' excellent series *Maths Call*.

9. A major problem in teaching is that there are so many reasons for using your voice that children stop listening to it. Look for ways of using visual channels of communication for classroom organisation and behaviour management:
   - use a physical signal for calling the class to order, such as holding one arm in the air, to which pupils respond by settling down and returning the signal;
   - for classroom routines or rules you frequently need to repeat, make a poster, then just point;
   - for pupils who constantly need reminding about how to behave, make visual cue cards for a teaching assistant to hold up.

10. The earlier we begin to develop speaking and listening skills, the greater the advantages – for children, teachers and schools. See page 80, and resources in Appendix 5.

Spoken and Written Language Patterns

Written language is more

EXPLICIT

ORGANISED

COHERENT

than spoken language

Differences between spoken and written language

It's now well established that written language is very different from the spoken version. Speech is usually interactive – we bat words and phrases back and forth – and produced within a shared context, so it's fragmented, disorganised and a great deal of meaning goes by on the nod. In fact, you can get by in speech without ever forming a sentence, or at least only very simple ones. To make links between ideas, speakers tend to use very simple connectives, like the ubiquitous *and* or, to denote sequence, *and then*.

Writing, on the other hand, is produced for an unknown, unseen audience, who may have no background knowledge at all about the subject. It is therefore explicit, complex, crafted, requiring a wider vocabulary than speech and organisation into sentences for clarity. The sentences become increasingly complex as the writer expresses increasingly complex ideas, and require a wide range of 'connectives' to show how these ideas relate to each other.

When they start writing, young children are unaware of these differences and produce 'speech written down'. We must develop their awareness of written language patterns, starting with the concept of 'the sentence' and gradually building up their capacity to vary and control sentence structure, fill in background detail, and link ideas coherently.

Children who learn to read quickly and fluently are at an advantage here: they internalise written language patterns the same way they internalised spoken language patterns – through exposure. Those children who don't learn to read easily (and the increasing number of children who can read but don't) have more difficulty. But if introduced to these structures, and given opportunities to practise them in writing, they too can learn to manipulate and control language to express their ideas.

The interface between speech and writing

As children become increasingly literate, these written language patterns also begin to inform their speech – it's a cyclical process: speech informs writing, which then informs speech, which informs writing, and so on. In general, the more accomplished the writer, the better equipped he or she will be to 'talk like a book'. And the capacity for 'literate talk' is perhaps the most important literacy skill of all.

Until the late 19th century, this interface between speech and writing was universally acknowledged. From the time of the Ancient Greeks, rhetoric (reading aloud, speaking persuasively) was considered as essential a part of education as reading and writing – perhaps even more so. However, the introduction of universal state education automatically meant large classes in which speech for the many was not deemed possible, and the literacy curriculum was restricted to reading and writing. Throughout the twentieth century, educators have concentrated their attention on literacy, at the expense of oracy. Today, even teachers who provide spoken language activities seldom consider the aspect of 'literate talk'.

We believe the loss of this 'fourth R' has been a damaging development in two major ways:

- the neglect of the virtuous circle (speech to writing to speech and so on) has probably contributed to our present difficulties with the teaching of writing;
- all children deserve to be able speak up and speak out, with literate control of their language.

The latter point is important both for reasons of personal development (social skills, self-confidence and self-esteem), and for social and economic purposes (from the ability to tell jokes and anecdotes to success in interviews, tutorials and presentations in the workplace). Indeed, as multimedia proliferate, the ability to 'talk like a book' will probably become much more important than the ability to write like one. For this reason, we believe it is important to distinguish between **talk for learning** and **talk for writing**.

Talk for Learning

Talk as part of imaginative engagement:

Drama and role-play

Puppets, prompts and props

Corners, learning areas and 'virtual contexts'

Talk around first hand experiences:

Interviews and visits

Making pictures, models, collages, tapes, videos...

active learning of all kinds

Storytelling

Directed talk linked to learning:

Regular paired talk

Group discussion – open-ended questions, problem-solving

Show and tell

Prepared presentations and assemblies

Literacy: what works? © Sue Palmer and Pie Corbett, Nelson Thornes, 2003

Howard Gardner once claimed that we remember 20% of what we see, 30% of what we hear, 40% of what we say, 50% of what we do... and 90% of what we hear, see, say and do. Most teachers would agree that the more actively involved children are in their learning, the more likely they are to engage with and retain what they have learned. Talk during learning also allows them to internalise new vocabulary and get to grips with the ideas and concepts underlying the subject matter, which will be vital when they come to write.

Imaginative engagement

Drama activities (see Appendix 1) allow all children to engage with the topic, even those who would generally take a back seat in class discussion. When in role, children are personally distanced from the words they utter, and thus freer to speak. Puppets have the same effect: indeed, children who have never spoken a word will often chatter happily through or to a puppet. Simple props relevant to the subject-matter (artefacts, models, cut-outs on sticks, soft toys) can have the same liberating effect, as well as providing a specific focus for talk. Props and role-play costumes can be kept in a learning 'corner', where pupils can browse or play, and where again they will often unselfconsciously engage with the topic.

Sadly, though these techniques are generally widely used in Early Years, as pupils grow older teachers feel they are no longer appropriate. But all three strategies, adapted as appropriate, work throughout the primary school, and all create motivated, successful learners. Another source of 'learning contexts' appropriate for Key Stage 2 is the internet: browsing with a partner through an appropriate website provides many opportunities for theme-related talk.

First-hand experience

Active learning takes many forms: but it is generally engaging, enjoyable and a focus for purposeful talk. Maybe someone with first hand knowledge of the subject can come into school to be interviewed, or children despatched to visit them for homework (grandparents are often a wonderful source of information). If there isn't a suitable museum or place of interest to visit, perhaps you could just go for a walk to hunt for evidence or examples of whatever you're studying in the local area. The more cross-curricular links you can make with art, music, and DT, the more opportunities you create for talk about or around the topic. Children may also have considerable knowledge on a topic themselves if you're able to plumb it – storytelling techniques (see Appendices 2 and 5) are useful for eliciting children's accounts of their own experience.

Directed talk

The activities listed above provide vehicles for generalised talk for learning. You can narrow the conversational focus through opportunities for paired talk (see page 59 – section 4) or group discussion. The latter is most productive when based around open-ended questions, and there is much helpful advice on developing pupils' discussion techniques and devising suitable questions in the video pack *Thinking Allowed*. Other ways of directing attention towards specific aspects of the subject are Show and Tell sessions, in which individual pupils give prepared talks about an object or picture, and prepared presentations (to the class or other pupils in the school).

In the 'two horses' model for teaching cross-curricular writing (page 44) we recommend providing speaking and listening activities at both text and sentence level. The activities above are 'text level talk' involving spoken language patterns (see page 63). However, feedback to the class from paired or group work, prepared talks for Show and Tell and other formal presentations can also be used to develop 'sentence level talk' (written language patterns), as shown in the next section.

Talk for Writing

LISTEN → IMITATE → INNOVATE → INVENT

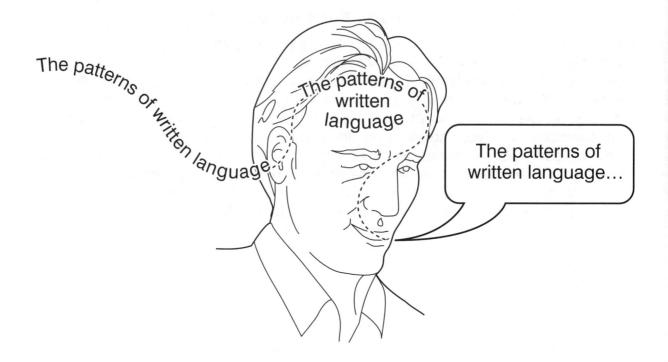

An example of a 'speaking frame'

.... and .... are alike in several ways.

One similarity is that ....

Another way in which they are alike is ....

They are both ....

A further feature they have in common is ....

In previous chapters we have referred to the developmental model for acquisition of spoken language: first children **listen** to adult speakers and **imitate** elements of their speech; later they begin to **innovate** on these language patterns; finally they use all this language data to **invent** their own expressions. However, in writing, which is a very different form of language from the spoken version, teachers often expect children to skip the earlier stages and go straight to invention. We are therefore increasingly convinced that children benefit from mirroring stages in this developmental model in order to absorb the patterns of written language, for use both in writing and in 'literate talk'.

Listen

Children need opportunities to hear good writing read aloud, to become familiar with the rhythms and patterns of written sentences. We have already commended the tradition of 'storytime' for developing the imagination and training listening skills. As well as stories and poems, we should also read aloud non-fiction books or magazine articles.

Some teachers play story or poetry tapes to accompany quiet activities, like art and DT. We could also recommend these to parents for long car journeys or if they are unable to read bedtime stories themselves: a tape recorder in the bedroom would be greatly preferable to a TV. Schools could encourage the use of tapes by organising a tape library.

Imitate

Children also need to read aloud themselves to hear literate language patterns produced from their own mouths; to know how standard English and sophisticated vocabulary feels; to respond physically to the ebb and flow of well-constructed sentences. Young children can internalise narrative patterns by joining in with familiar stories until they are practically 'reading along' with the whole text, or by constant retelling of a familiar tale. Older children should have many opportunities to read with expression but, as there's little time for this within a guided reading session, perhaps paired reading (reading with a partner – a page or paragraph each) could be used instead. With a little training (see for instance Keith Topping's book *Thinking, Reading, Writing*) paired reading could become a regular activity during independent time. Children also need opportunities to learn poems or passages by heart for performance (see ESB, below).

Innovate

The language play described on page 43 allows children to innovate on written language patterns, and also to hear certain language constructions repeated frequently by peers. In terms of story text, there are many suggestions for activities on page 51 and in Appendix 2. Another way of encouraging innovation on written language patterns is the use of 'speaking frames'. Literacy consultants in Stockton-on-Tees have produced a book of 'speech frames' for Year 6, based on an Anthony Browne book (*Talk First: Voices in the Park*). Sue has been working on a similar idea for cross-curricular teaching in Key Stage 2, tackling major cohesive elements in non-fiction texts (*Speaking Frames*). The frame opposite, for instance, can be used by a group to feed back to the class after open-ended discussion establishing similarities between two objects or texts. After several groups have fed back, the language structures should be familiar and can hopefully be accessed by pupils in their writing and formal talk.

Invent

Prepared presentations or 'speeches' (say in debates or class/school council meetings) are vehicles for fusing written and spoken language activities, and for practising literate talk. Opportunities arise naturally out of the curriculum (storytelling, Show and Tell sessions, group presentations to the class), but participation in a specific speech programme, such as that produced by the English Speaking Board, allows pupils to hone speech and presentation skills. The ESB course includes a prepared reading or recitation, an illustrated presentation on a subject of the pupil's choice, and a question session on the content of this talk.

Where Do We Go Next?

Change the ethos

It is clear from teachers' responses on page 58 that the ethos in English primary schools is inimical to the development of children's spoken language. This is a long-standing problem, perhaps related to the origins of universal elementary education, perhaps to a national characteristic (this is, after all, the country where 'children should be seen and not heard'). However, in recent years it has been exacerbated by the tests-and-targets culture, the emphasis in the NLS framework on pencil-and-paper work, and Ofsted's thirst for 'evidence', which teachers have taken to mean marks on paper rather than evidence of progress.

As we move into a multimedia age, in which the uses of literacy have already changed considerably from those of a previous generation, the capacity to speak well is ever more important. If, as we have argued, oracy and literacy are also mutually interdependent, this anti-talk ethos is probably also damaging literacy standards. It is therefore a matter of urgency that we break the hold of the ethos. Primary schools must become places where speaking and listening is, for every pupil, at the heart of the learning process.

As well as clear messages in this direction from the National Primary Strategy and Ofsted, teachers also need support in developing teaching strategies which genuinely embed language and listening in the learning process (not just the encouragement of superficial chitchat). Such a change of ethos and practice cannot be achieved through government dictats, scripted lessons or endless 'assessment procedures', tactics which have already proved to do considerably more harm than good. In the end, the only way forward may be to trust the teaching profession to do something about it themselves, through developing a culture of research, innovation and dissemination of ideas to colleagues (see page 84).

Revise Early Years policy

We have already noted that the introduction of formal 'pencil and paper work' at too early an age can be damaging to children. This is particularly the case in terms of speaking and listening, and current practice in many nursery and reception classes is causing concern to speech and language therapists as well as to the many Early Years specialists we meet.

In other European countries a highly structured course of child-friendly speaking and listening activities between the ages of 3 and 6 paves the way for later success in formal learning. Early attention to speaking and listening also develops children's attentional skills, self confidence and social competence. We believe that many 'attention deficit' problems are simply the result of poor listening skills when the child first entered school or nursery.

One very important strand in changing the ethos of primary education would be to change our approach to Early Years (see page 80).

Revive the Fourth R

Simply giving more attention to speaking and listening is not enough. We need specifically to encourage pupils' awareness and control of **literate talk**, which means developing oral activities that use the patterns of written language. Over time, this should have the direct benefit of improving both spoken language and writing.

Planning, Assessment, Marking and SATs

English children are the most tested children in the world. It begins as they enter school and continues relentlessly. Yet many teachers feel that the testing system does not accurately reflect children's performance and that league tables are unfair because they do not demonstrate what differences schools make, based as they are on a narrow view of education.

The greatest problem with tests used to publicly rank schools and teachers is that the test inevitably drives what is taught. If you want people to do something, then test them – link it to their pay, their public standing, their Ofsted analysis – and inevitably they will focus upon achieving in the test. The climate of testing and ranking schools has had a negative effect on the broad aims of education and needs to be refined.

There is a similar problem with planning. The National Literacy Strategy's early training materials provided examples of planning which were overcrowded with excessive detail. This led to the ludicrous situation of confident teachers wasting time filling in hugely detailed planning forms so that the head teacher could put them in a file, to show to the local adviser or Ofsted team (and it seems that there is nothing some Ofsted teams like more than a fat file full of plans and assessments!).

Planning and assessment have thus been hijacked in the name of 'accountability' and used to rank children, teachers and schools. As a profession, we need to reclaim both processes for pedagogic reasons, to help us teach purposefully and assess the results of our teaching. The 2003 QCA assessment focuses, which underpin the mark schemes for national tests (see example on page 76) are surprisingly helpful in determining what makes a good reader or a good writer. While it will take time for all teachers to become familiar with these, and with the mark schemes, we should aim to use them to improve our teaching – while bearing in mind that there's a lot more to reading and writing than performance on a test.

At the same time, we should also recognise that teachers, as public servants, are accountable: standardised tests let the public know how we as a profession are doing, and allow schools to compare their own achievement with that of others.

Planning for literacy	70
Making marking work	72
Hitting literacy targets	74
National testing and league tables	76
Where do we go next?	78

Planning for Literacy

LONG TERM

- blocks and sequences – reading, oracy and writing

MEDIUM TERM

- build in authors, poets and texts
- move non-fiction to fit with the rest of the curriculum
- flexible week – respond to children's needs
- save time – use ICT/annotate existing plans
- share out planning – avoid rewriting plans
- standard format not necessary – just common elements, e.g. objectives, simple record keeping

WEEKLY PLANNING

- confident teachers – use lesson notes
- allow for spontaneity and flexible timing
- focus on learning not delivery
- use multi-sensory teaching
- be prepared not overplanned
- planning leads to plenary

Ofsted looks for – clear learning objectives; how these will be achieved.

Inspectors will not expect to find a particular model or format for planning; they will be much more interested in the impact of planning on your teaching and the children's learning.

Excellence and Enjoyment (DfES)

Long-term planning

Outline plans for each year should:

- be based on blocks of work built around specific text types;
- have clear learning objectives;
- identify how end-of-unit assessment will take place;
- be stored on the computer, needing only minor tweaking each year – in the light of the impact of previous teaching, and the needs of the present class.

The length of each block needs careful thought and relates to the demands of the text type and the children's familiarity with that type of language. Blocks of work should cluster objectives that relate to each other – and be divided into sequences for teaching. Blocks should provide opportunities for plenty of reading experience of the text type and of 'talking' the text type before writing.

Mid-term planning

Mid-term plans should include a school grid showing which authors, poets and texts are being studied, so that the school can gather relevant resources over the years. Non-fiction blocks should be moved to fit in with the rest of the curriculum, trips and celebrations so that literacy-skills teaching can be immediately applied. Save time by sharing out planning and annotating existing plans. Standard formats are not necessary though it helps if key elements are included by everyone, e.g. clear learning objectives, a simple record-keeping system.

Weekly planning

Where teachers are confident in their subject matter and have internalised fundamental patterns for structuring learning, they do not need to write lengthy lesson plans. A brief weekly overview of what's planned is sufficient. The teacher's time should be spent on preparation rather than completing planning formats.

Excessive concern about day-by-day coverage of objectives can mean teachers lose sight of children's needs or the importance of securing learning. Over-planning the week's work may provide a sense of security but can also lead to inflexibility. Sometimes lessons need to speed up, on other occasions the teacher may need to revisit an aspect of learning. We must be prepared to alter plans in relation to what happens. Put simply: what should we do if we teach something and the work is poor or the children just haven't applied what we taught? All too often there is a mad dash on to the next objective. It might be more sensible to revisit the work and be a tad more insistent!

Spontaneity and flexibility

Teachers should not adhere so rigidly to plans that they cannot be spontaneous – many teachers say their best lessons have been carried out on a whim. When something arises – a local or national event, a child brings something in to school – and the children are interested, teachers must feel free to seize the moment and use these stimuli to develop talk, reading or writing. Learning takes place when we are motivated.

We all learn in different ways. Multi-sensory teaching means using a mixture of visual, aural/oral, cognitive and kinaesthetic techniques. It means we must plan more drama, listening to tapes, watching video clips, using first-hand experiences and so forth.

Many schools are still timetabled for an hour of literacy, but an hour may not be long enough – especially for drama or writing. Teachers should make these decisions for themselves in relation to the objectives and the class. We remember the days when you could send a runner to the head saying *Sorry to miss your assembly but we are writing a story and it's going well*. If creativity matters, you don't dare interrupt the writing. You take a late break instead!

Making Marking Work

Sample A: Y2 writing in R.E. + teacher's comment

One day Jairus little girl became ill. She died but Jesus brought her back again to life again.

*Excellent 2 **

Sample B: Year 6 – Teacher's comment

This is a very mature and entertaining biography that contains all the right ingredients. Well done.

1. Start a new line and indent when doing quotes.
2. Keep all verbs in the past tense.

Sample C: Year 3 – part of a story + marking

The cat <u>went</u> down to the bottom of
the garden it sat there and waited
the dog <u>came up</u> the path it was <u>going</u>
so quiet because it wanted to <u>get</u> the cat ...

Sample D: Year 6 – marking + child's amendments

Daniel and I crept cautiously
I got back in the garden. <u>Me and daniel</u> <u>walked</u>
dug
? over to the Dug up ground. I latched the hook in
heaved. It
and <u>pulled</u> it was very heavy so I got Daniel to help.

Literacy: what works? © Sue Palmer and Pie Corbett, Nelson Thornes, 2003

Making marking work

If we are going to spend time marking then it must lead to improving children's work. However, we spend hours growling, hissing and spitting from the margins – often to little effect. And some children keep repeating the same errors continually ... We need strategies to make marking quicker and more effective.

Working with the class to draw up a list of criteria (a 'marking ladder' or 'toolkit') BEFORE writing, e.g. *To write a good opening you need to* ... helps the children write and focuses marking. When the class write, ask a few children to write straight onto an OHT or one child to type straight onto the interactive whiteboard. This can be used in the plenary or at the start of the next session for evaluation and 'polishing'. In the end, children need to be able to revise their own writing independently – improving the content and making their work more accurate.

Of course, marking has other key functions. It should make us think about what we need to teach next. It is worth having a notepad beside you when marking so you can make notes about common aspects that need improving. You can also look for a few effective examples to show the whole class for discussion (again put these on to OHTs). Feedback from marking should be planned into the next session – and the children should get used to responding to the marking, making immediate improvements where the teacher indicates.

Finally, marking helps us to pick up a sense of how successful our teaching has been. It's pretty easy to spot when an activity has flopped! This can help us readjust our plans and teaching.

Highlights

Speed up the process of marking by using a highlighter to indicate effective parts of children's writing. Identify where a specific lesson objective has been achieved or progress made. As children gain confidence, they can highlight where they think they have achieved a specific objective or target. Older pupils may write a comment before handing work in, drawing your attention to what they are pleased with – or an aspect that they want you to look at. Ask them to tick their 'best' bit and bracket with a question mark a section that they are concerned about (see sample D).

Writing comments

Not every piece of writing requires a comment. Where a comment is made try the following:

- Use the child's name – address the writer (sadly missing in samples A and B).
- Be specific when commenting about a key aspect that is effective, e.g. *This contains all the right ingredients*. Avoid comments such as *Excellent* (sample A) – which may be kindness but is not effective marking (What aspect is excellent?).
- Note one aspect that needs to be worked on next time, using some such phrase as *Next time....*, e.g. *Next time keep all the verbs in the past tense* (sample B). When work is returned the children read their comments and sign. They may write a response – perhaps commenting on what they have learned from the marking, e.g. *I now see how I should set out the dialogue*.
- Use proactive marking (as in sample C), identifying where the child needs to make improvements (see page 74). In sample D, you can see the changes made by the child to one section he had bracketed for the teacher to look at.

Hitting Literacy Targets

Symbols for annotating children's writing

Content

Squiggle under a word = weak word – try again!

^ = insert a good word, phrase or clause.

R = repetition – you find it and change it.

( ) = rewrite this bit so that I can understand it

↗ – insert extra section, e.g. develop argument more.

? = something wrong here – you find it and put it right.

Circle whole section of text – rewrite this section here.

Spelling

Sircle a word = spelling that needs changing (common words and patterns that have been taught).

Punctuation

■ The 'bright but careless' writer – write the number of errors at the top of the page.

■ Less confident writers – work in pairs, re-reading and inserting punctuation.

■ Least confident writers – X in the margin = full stop missing.

Next time targets

Every school sets targets. Some children have so many targets that they can't remember them all! Setting targets on their own doesn't magically help children's work improve. Bear in mind the following:

- The targets need discussing when work is returned.
- Remind the children before they write, halfway through writing and just before the end – have they remembered to focus upon their target (because you will be looking for this when you are marking)?
- It is easy to set targets for obvious aspects of writing such as – spelling, punctuation and handwriting. Don't forget developing the quality of the writing. Familiarity with QCA SAT mark schemes helps you understand progress in writing and thus set better targets (see over page).
- Finally, some teachers set individual targets. This may seem ideal but it means that you cannot teach the targets, let alone pick up on them in your marking. Try setting the same specific targets for two or three groups of children – this is manageable for teaching.

Target setting can be a dynamic part of marking that helps to focus the children on what they need to think about in order to improve. It is at its most effective where the teacher is good at assessment and has in mind where the children need to be by the end of the year. This is linked to expectation – getting a strong sense of what good writing and reading are like for different year groups.

Focused marking

Many teachers mark using the scatter-gun approach – any old thing that crops up comes under the line of fire! Focus your marking as this makes it quicker and more effective:

- Mark to the lesson objective.
- Pick up on progress towards targets.
- Focus on where the children have ticked or bracketed aspects they are pleased with – or concerned about.
- Use marking to insist on basic aspects that have been taught but not learned, e.g. using a full stop!

Focus on a section or aspect of the text, e.g. the opening, the dialogue, the use of complex sentences. It is handy if the children are very clear of the focus before they write. This can be written the top of the page as a reminder, e.g. *I need to write an ending that shows how the character has changed*.

Annotating writing

When marking, annotate the writing to identify where it might be improved. When the work is returned the class spend five minutes or so 'polishing' their writing, on their own or with response partners, making improvements where you have indicated. Try the following routine:

- Return all books.
- Children read comments, sign and write response if they wish.
- Show a child's example on OHT or interactive whiteboard.
- Author reads aloud, and identifies aspects they like and areas that need improvement.
- Class comment on strengths and make suggestions for improvement to author.
- Teacher focuses class on objective or aspect of progress.
- All children polish their own writing, making changes where the teacher's marking has indicated.

National Testing and League Tables

QCA's assessment focuses for writing

COMPOSITION AND EFFECT

1. Write imaginative, interesting and thoughtful texts.

2. Produce texts which are appropriate to task, reader and purpose.

Adaptation
Viewpoint
Style

TEXT STRUCTURE AND ORGANISATION

3. Organise and present whole texts effectively, structuring information, ideas and events.

Coherence
Cohesion

4. Construct paragraphs and use cohesion between paragraphs.

SENTENCE STRUCTURE AND PUNCTUATION

5. Vary sentences for clarity, purpose and effect.

Variety
Clarity
Accuracy

6. Write with technical accuracy of syntax and punctuation in phrases, clauses and sentences.

WORD LEVEL

7. Select appropriate and effective vocabulary.

8. Use correct spelling.

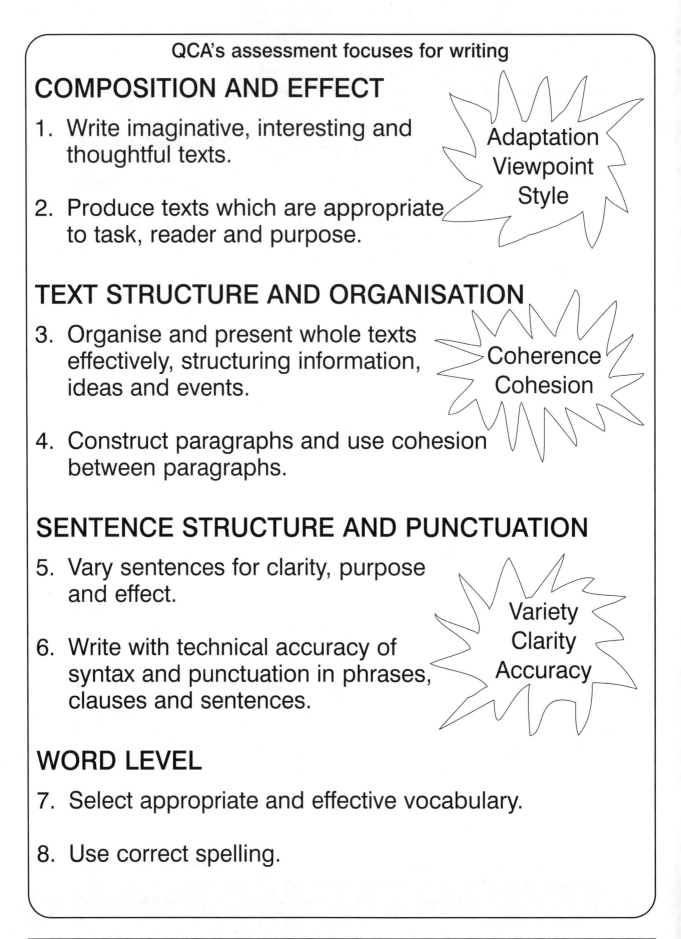

National testing

Given the wide differences in the quality of education that children experience, it seems only right that national testing of some form be used. It focuses us all on ensuring that children have adequate literacy skills to take advantage of secondary education and to enhance their life chances. QCA's assessment focuses are helpful in terms of planning and teaching (see Writing Assessment focuses opposite), and tests based on these should also be helpful. However, difficulties arise because the tests have become such a public issue, with schools' and teachers' reputations resting on the outcome.

This means that concerns about the tests themselves assume huge importance. For instance, many teachers feel the KS2 tests disadvantage slow paced readers and writers. Every year there are some children (slow, careful readers or writers) who only manage to complete three quarters of the paper – often getting everything right up to that point. Given longer time, they would complete the test and provide a more accurate picture of their ability. Perhaps there should be an upper limit of, say, one hour for completion in both the reading and longer writing tasks.

There are many more worries over the testing of writing, including issues such as:

- weak or inconsistent marking;
- quality and range of the tasks set (input from a panel of teachers/writers/ researchers might help ensure tasks are sufficiently stimulating);
- inconsistency between KS1 and KS2 testing procedures (KS1 have a term to prepare, while KS2's tests are unseen), which means children seem to go backwards on the Year 3 optional SATs.

Further concerns arise, particularly regarding Key Stage 1, about the pressures on young children caused by high-stakes testing, and the effect that so much emphasis on pencil-and-paper work has on the ethos of early years' provision. In the circumstances, we believe QCA should look seriously at whether KS1 tests are worth keeping, and at making further refinements to the KS2 testing regime.

League tables

Originally, the SATs were meant to help teachers see what children had attained and decide therefore what needed to be done next. Sadly, they have grown into a way of publicly ranking schools in league tables. It is the use of SAT results by Ofsted and the league tables that engenders so much pressure. Local papers love to make a story out of who is bottom and who is top. The anxiety caused by this public ranking leads to narrowing of the curriculum and an emphasis on coaching and boosting children to achieve higher marks.

We would also query whether league tables show an honest picture. For instance, if you set the children's VRQ scores (verbal reasoning quotient) against their SAT scores you can produce a totally different sort of league table, showing how well children are doing given their verbal reasoning ability. In one county when this was done, a school that had always been top of the league table with 100% at Level 4 suddenly dropped 350 places! The children may well have attained Level 4 and 5 – but given their high VRQs, they would have gained higher scores in almost any other school in the county.

The tests, targets and league table ethos is a leftover from the regime of Chris Woodhead. Since the arrival of David Bell at Ofsted there have been signs of the beginnings of a more humane and balanced approach to helping schools provide a quality education. We hope over time to see this influencing the testing regime as well.

Where Do We Go Next?

Keep planning purposeful

Teachers who lack subject confidence may need to plan assiduously. Those who are confident should be able to make 'teacherly notes' and use these for teaching. Currently many schools expect experienced and talented teachers to write down the level of detail that is appropriate for students in training. This is a waste of their time.

Drop Key Stage 1 SATs

There are so many problems around Key Stage 1 SATs, that it would probably be better to abandon them, as has already been done in Wales. Schools would still need to assess children's progress in reading and spelling, but this could be done using standardised tests, without all the fuss and fretting associated with SATs. Writing could be assessed by the teacher on the basis of a portfolio of work built up over the year. This would require strong moderation from the LEA, but would give a much better picture of the child's ability than the current 'one-off' piece of writing (often based on a great deal of rehearsal).

The results of KS1 assessments should be made available to parents, but not published or publicised in any form.

Refine Key Stage 2 SATs

Most problems at Key Stage 2 seem to relate to the writing SAT. These could be ameliorated by balancing SAT results with a portfolio of children's writing, assessed by the teacher, in order to arrive at a broad consensus of the child's level. As well as seeming fairer to the children, this would also help overcome the problems of sending on to secondary school children who seem to be at one level when actually they are not! The tests themselves also need further refinement, and the time allocations should be reviewed: at present there is too much of a premium on speed.

League tables

League tables should be dropped. Parents can find each school's information by asking. We need more information that shows 'value-added'. And we should all value much more the whole child – the ability to get on with others, kindness, dance, art, football, being a librarian... Education is is not only about attaining a Level 4 – it's about the human spirit and how we cherish it. Politicians, remember that.

Post Script

```
                    Underachievement
        Teacher
        training              Inclusion


                        Early
                        Years          Consultants
    Multimedia

                        Balance
        Meaning-
        making
```

We have attempted in the preceding chapters to sum up some important points about the teaching of literacy, especially the many changes in teaching practice that have taken place in the last five years. However, literacy is a vast subject, stretching its tentacles into practically every corner of the primary curriculum and beyond. In the space available we have often done no more than scratch the surface of a topic – and there are many other important areas on which we haven't even touched.

This final chapter, therefore, is a collection of short essays acting as a postscript to the rest of the book:

- some offer a brief overview of areas we haven't covered;
- others draw together threads left dangling unsatisfactorily elsewhere;
- each of them offers suggestions for 'where we might go next'.

We are only too aware that the pace of educational change often renders commentary redundant. The vast amount of change chronicled in the preceding pages is testimony to the speed with which literacy teaching has developed over the last five years. As we were writing this book, during two months in spring 2003, there were several significant shifts in policy which will have their impact on teachers in the coming academic year. By the time the book is published, there may well have been many more.

However, the very volatility of our educational world increases the importance of stopping on occasion to stand back and reflect. 2003 is a significant year, in that the original Literacy Strategy has been laid to rest, and the Primary Strategy is rising from its ashes. We hope this personal snapshot of the pedagogy and practice of literacy teaching in Britain will enable teachers and others to reflect productively before, as always, we all move on.

The Early Years	80
'The long tail of underachievement'	81
Language, learning and meaning-making	82
Literacy and multimedia	83
Teacher training	84
Consultants, LEA and Uncle Tom Cobley	85
Inclusion and 'individual teaching'	86
Maintaining a balance	87

The Early Years

Over the last few years, the 'pencil and paper' culture engendered by national testing has extended downwards in many schools to influence practice in reception, and sometimes even nursery classes. It has been compounded by the NLS literacy objectives for reception, including the requirement that the Literacy Hour structure is in place for all children by the end of the year. Many children are now expected to engage in formal literacy lessons long before they are ready to benefit from them.

With any luck, changes to the Key Stage 1 testing regime and the establishment of the Foundation Stage curriculum will enable Early Years practitioners to re-establish a proper 'foundation ethos' in nursery and reception, in which the skills and concepts required for reading and writing are developed through activities appropriate to the age-group. In such an ethos, it should be possible to interpret NLS objectives in a more child-friendly way. However, even with excellent nursery and reception practice, in many schools the majority of pupils will not achieve all the Early Learning Goals for language, communication and literacy by the end of the reception year. For them, the foundation ethos needs to extend upwards, into Year 1 (see *Smooth Transitions* by Ros Bayley and Sally Featherstone).

Towards a transition year

It is very difficult, however, for schools to take this step, as they are obliged by law to provide the National Curriculum from the beginning of Year 1. This is generally interpreted as meaning that formal literacy teaching should begin in Year 1, whether children are ready for it or not (and when many summerborns have had only one term in reception). As long as this state of affairs continues, large numbers of children will continue to fall at the first fence in their literacy learning, and we will continue to waste time and resources on endless 'catch-up' packages.

For the majority of children to achieve the Early Learning Goals through activities appropriate to their needs, schools need greater flexibility about the onset of the National Curriculum. The Foundation Stage profile now provides sound evidence upon which schools could choose to decide when formal learning should begin, for all or some children, at any time between the end of reception and the start of Year 2. We believe that government should recognise Year 1 as a transition period between the Foundation Curriculum and the National Curriculum, in which practice will vary depending on the circumstances of individual schools and, perhaps, specific cohorts within schools.

Preparation for literacy

However, in order to prepare children for formal literacy, Early Years practitioners need more guidance than that in the Early Learning Goals and the Foundation Profile. They need to know more about listening skills, spoken language development, phonemic awareness, the physical skills required for handwriting and the development of awareness of print and written language conventions. They also need advice and resources to provide the sorts of experiences through which little children will best acquire these skills and concepts – including an emphasis on music, song and oral work.

There is a further benefit to be had from these changes. Environmental and cultural changes in the final decades of the 20th century have meant we can no longer expect children's listening skills to be well developed by the time they reach primary school. Speech therapists believe that more emphasis on oral work in the Early Years, including the specific development of listening skills, would have a beneficial effect on children's attention span, social skills and self esteem, all important contributors to the type of behaviour needed for school-based learning. A more coherent approach to our preparation for literacy could also prevent the development of many behaviour problems, and benefit all children's learning, across the curriculum and throughout their school careers.

'The Long Tail of Underachievement'

The National Literacy Strategy was set up in response to government concern about 'the long tail of underachievement' in English schools. According to the psychologists, between five and ten per cent of children within a normal population might be expected to have significant difficulties in reading and writing during their primary years. By the mid-1990s the figure for struggling readers in England was nearer to 40 per cent.

Three waves of provision

The Strategy's answer is three 'waves' of provision. The first wave, directed at all children, was the Literacy Hour with all its attendant pedagogy and practice, described as 'Quality First Teaching'. The second wave of 'catch-up' programmes was aimed at picking up children who had begun to fall behind. *Additional Literacy Support* (ALS) for children in Year 3 and 4 was introduced in 1999. It was no coincidence that many of its beneficiaries would sit their SATs in 2002, the first of the government's 'target years'. In common with the next two second-wave programmes – *Early Learning Support* (ELS) for Year 1 pupils and *Further Learning Support* (FLS) for Year 5 pupils – it was designed to be delivered by specially trained teaching assistants. These TAs were seen as 'smart weapons', trained to deal with a particular type of pupil. The third wave of provision is for children with clearly identified special needs.

Prevention better than cure?

While we welcome 'catch-up' programmes for children whose difficulties have previously gone unrecognised, we wonder if it might be more sensible to 'catch' and prevent literacy problems before they begin. The long tail of under-achievement is composed broadly of two groups of children: those from economically-deprived backgrounds, and boys. There is gathering evidence that both groups may be better served by delaying the onset of formal literacy education, and spending more time on preparation for literacy.

International research studies show that the famous 'gender gap' (girls out-performing boys in literacy throughout KS1-3) is significantly greater in those countries where compulsory school attendance begins at 5, rather than 6 or 7. It seems clear that the later maturation of boys means they are generally less suited than girls to an early start. By insisting that all children begin formal literacy learning at the age of 5 (and often earlier) we may well be sentencing many boys to long-term failure.

Similarly, children from less advantaged backgrounds often arrive at school with less well-developed language skills than others. The problems with listening and language described on page 80 often tend to be more pronounced in this group, who would particularly benefit from more oral work and listening development before formal education begins.

Teaching how to learn

However, no matter how hard we work to prevent failure, every class seems to contain a few children who appear able to acquire basic skills but whose progress is nevertheless slow. Teaching should also address their specific needs. We believe there are two main problems, the first of which is that they don't know how to listen and/or concentrate. As we point out on page 61, for many children nowadays listening is a skill that has to be taught. Similarly, in a quick-fix, multimedia age, concentration does not always come naturally and has to be developed, through gradual training. The second problem is poor motivation. Dealing with this can be the most rewarding part of teaching – it can take time finding out what will light the spark, but it's great when you succeed!

Language, Learning and Meaning-making

The desire to communicate basic needs is totally instinctive. Language itself is learned through imitation, repetition and purposeful interaction with proficient language users. The minds of primary children are geared up to learn language. The language they are best at is their own local dialect, influenced by home and their immediate peers. They are very skilled at this local language. This does not mean that they cannot broaden their repertoire. Indeed, we all know what happens if you take a 7-year-old and place them in French family and school for 9 months. They become bi-lingual! In school, we expect children to step beyond their local language and become adept at other varieties – narrative, persuasive, explanatory and so on.

The issue for many children is not that they cannot speak or write in other registers. It is insufficient experience of the language, a lack of purpose and audience. When these conditions are met, children strive to use language, at the edge of their competence. Keen to acquire new vocabulary, they attempt new sentence structures and even develop the skills of rhetoric.

In the Strategy emphasis was placed upon the need to immerse children in different types of written language, to use models, to demonstrate and scaffold learning. However, the need to provide purposes for talking and writing, so that children have something to say and the desire to communicate, was insufficiently addressed. The need to ensure an audience so children would strive to craft language, adopting an appropriate register, was also underplayed.

This often led to rather bland interpretation of objectives, lacking any real motivation. Many writing sessions began with no stimulus other than the model text. Lessons become 'worthy but dull'. The recent clarion call from the DfES to put the fun back into primary education picks up on this point. Primary teachers need to use their own creativity and imagination to provide engaging, imaginative starting points that motivate children to write – as well as providing audiences for what is spoken and written. We use language most effectively when the topic is something we know about and it matters to us. They have to 'feel' something: e.g.

1. First hand experience – visits, visitors, location writing, candle poems
2. Drama – hot-seating, role-play, acting out stories, putting the wolf on trial
3. Visual triggers – paintings, collections of objects, observing leaf skeletons
4. Oral triggers – music, storytelling, listening to a poet read
5. Imaginative set-ups – a class receiving a letter from the King
6. Building contexts – creating the bears' cave, a teddy bear picnic, singing growly bear songs, going on a bear hunt.

Providing audience, e.g.

1. Talk – debates, sharing anecdotes, being agony aunt to Flat Stanley
2. Paper publishing – regular anthologies, homemade books, origami books
3. Using technology – websites, emailing a newsboard, taping a poetry programme
4. Displays – haiku and paintings, newsboard for the old folks' home.

Finally, we would claim that experience only comes into being when it is expressed in words. The relationship between experience, language, thinking and doing is so important that oracy needs to play a central role in all lessons. It is how we bring into being what we almost know and then extend what we have learned through interacting with others.

Literacy and Multimedia

Despite the fact that we live in a multimedia world, literacy teaching (and the National Literacy Strategy) has remained firmly rooted in 'old-fashioned' book-based, pencil-and-paper literacy. While agreeing that these basic skills are still essential, and will continue to be so no matter how technology proliferates, we believe literacy teaching should also take account of video, audio and information technology.

Television, video, DVD and audio

In the early days of NLS, teachers were warned against using educational TV programmes in the shared section of the Literacy Hour, thus leading to a sad decline in the use of TV and video. Both BBC and Channel 4 have produced some excellent resources, all linked to the requirements of the Strategy (have a look, for instance, at BBC's 2003 *Let's Write A Story* for KS2). Perhaps watching educational TV programmes could be reinstated as an independent activity, or fitted elsewhere in the curriculum. At the very least, it would be a productive way to spend wet playtimes.

The move from video to DVD will also make it easier for teachers to show useful snippets from TV programmes as part of their lesson, using a PC and projector – and the advent of the 'Digital Curriculum' will mean many such snippets should soon be available on the internet. Much useful audio material is already available on CD and the internet and can be useful in developing listening skills (see page 61).

Projectors and interactive whiteboards

The arrival of interactive whiteboards (or projectors linked to a PC, which is a much cheaper but slightly less whizzy-looking option) at last heralds a real change in attitudes to ICT for literacy teaching by making it available for shared work. Many teachers who have previously been unmoved by the potential of technology are suddenly seeing how it can be made to work for their classes. Shared reading on screen can be enhanced with highlighting and anotation; shared writing can become shared word-processing, demonstrating how a writer drafts, edits, and cuts-and-pastes during the actual process of composition; the bells and whistles on simple literacy programs can make skills work more attractive. However, when the whiteboard has been in the classroom for a while, it loses its shine. Most teachers tell us pupils can get bored with bells and whistles just as easily as with other resources. We need to vary our resources, integrating old and new technology to exploit the best of both worlds.

The 'classroom computer', ICT suites and tablet PCs

In the past, use of ICT by individuals or pairs of pupils has largely been confined to:

- specialist programs for those needing extra structured help in reading or spelling
- occasional word-processing or simple desktop publishing of specific pieces of writing
- 'talking stories' or skills-based games provided as a 'treat'.

However, the potential for shared on-screen literacy, with the teacher modelling a process, could lead to more general use in independent and guided time. As teachers' confidence grows, we hearing more reports of innovative work, such as pupils creating their own multimedia productions. Schools which have trialled wireless tablet PCs (see page 26) are impressed by these as a medium for both teacher and learners – although at present the price is prohibitive.

Teacher Training

Despite tighter control over what has to be learned during teacher training, some students still emerge feeling that they are ill prepared to teach the National Strategy. In our inservice sessions it is quite common for teachers to say, *I have learned more today than I did in four years of training*. However, we also meet many others who feel well prepared.

The main problems young teachers seem to have are a lack of knowledge of children's literature and a lack of confidence in their ability to write. Training should provide students with specific courses to bolster their knowledge of children's literature and develop their own ability to write creatively. Due to a prescribed curriculum, many students never have to create schemes of work or teaching ideas. This is a weakness in training, as schools who coped well with the Strategy were able to take the objectives and teach them in a lively, creative manner. It is this ability to take what looks dull and place it within a purposeful, motivating context that so often distinguishes those teachers who engage children from those who do not. Strengthening creativity, imagination and initiative should play a more central role in training. Teaching is not just a matter of 'delivering' a collection of given objectives.

We should establish strong school-based models of teacher education that provide time for students to investigate how children learn before practising teaching. Every student should work with at least one excellent teacher. Initial training should be followed by a mandatory 'return' to college after say three to five years, building on the experience of being a teacher. In initial training so much of value is lost due to the vagaries of youth, and sometimes because sessions do not seem essential to those whose prime concern is often rooted in the essential but superficial problems of getting children to line up quietly! Courses should also provide opportunity for philosophy and encourage discussion about the purpose and nature of education.

Partnerships between LEAs and training institutions should be established so that professional development becomes a seamless continuum. LEA personnel should be involved in initial training and benefit from the opportunity to research. Those involved in Higher Education should also play a stronger role in working with schools, taking more direct responsibility for the quality of education offered in their area.

Professional development

We believe that teachers are fundamentally creative, imaginative and intelligent people whose task is highly demanding and complex. Over the last five years there have been too many courses where 100 teachers are crammed into a room and told what to do. 'Death by powerpoint' will soon be put into medical dictionaries as an occupational affliction! Yes, we need research conferences and inspirational talks. However, smaller groups of teacher researchers, investigating aspects of local need, offer a powerful way forwards. Teachers should also be entitled to regular sabbatical leave every five to ten years in order to recharge the intellectual and creative batteries. More courses should offer input, time to try ideas out followed by a return session so that a commitment to use what has been learned becomes a regular part of training.

Consultants, LEA and Uncle Tom Cobley

Literacy consultants

The role of the literacy consultant is not easy. It takes some courage to walk in off the street and take someone else's class with teachers observing. The best consultants have managed to help schools develop, improving teaching through demonstration, peer teaching and observation. They have worked with schools to identify aspects that need improving, set up effective programmes and contribute to their development. Successful consultants often see themselves as being an extra member of staff.

There is no doubt that the Strategy would not have worked without the commitment of the literacy consultants. At their best, they have helped teachers see that their children can achieve beyond what the school had expected. One essential aspect of their work is to identify sympathetic members of staff and establish links within the school, so that once they have left, one or more 'advocates' will see the work continues. Consultants could play a stronger role in the future in setting up research and development projects between groups of school with similar needs and interests.

LEA advisers

The Strategy had a visible effect where local advisers attended training and monitored the introduction in schools. It was undermined where LEA advisers colluded with schools, sympathising with them about the 'unreasonable nature' of the demands. Effective teams helped schools to introduce the Strategy, monitored its impact and focused efforts on aspects that needed improvement in relation to the analysis of data and observation evidence. Where advisers allowed some flexibility, schools responded well to investigating new approaches to teaching. More blunt tactics, though possibly well-intended, sometimes backfired and built resentment. Interventions in some 'failing' schools by LEA advisers, especially where they were directly involved in running the school, demonstrated that in even the direst situation schools can flourish. Such talent needs tapping.

The historical role of LEA English adviser needs developing, linking it more strongly to research. Resources should be made available to allow for more localised initiatives, utilising the knowledge and creative resources of such key personnel. The Strategy would not have even been given space at the table if advisers had not been supportive. This was mainly due to the quality of, and respect given to, the NLS leadership.

Ofsted

At their worst, Ofsted inspections can slow a school's progress, cause undue panic and do not always identify the strengths and weaknesses of schools. Initially, inspection teams were often unhelpful – due to over-rigid interpretation, lack of subject knowledge by inspectors or well-meant but unfounded advice. The system relies too much on individuals working out of the back of their garage. We believe that inspection teams should be part of the profession, actively engaged on both sides of the coin – inspection and development. It is all too easy to sit on the edge sniping ... In the future, schools and LEAs need to refine their ability to effectively review their own work, perhaps publishing a report for parents once every three or four years. Schools could gather evidence, involving some external verification. Publication of reports that make it easy to identify teachers is destructive. Only summaries are needed.

The role of HMI with a specialism in English has been seriously undermined. This should be developed so that HMI takes a key role in securing a vision for literacy.

Inclusion and 'Individual Teaching'

We have not said much about Special Needs teaching or teaching children with English as an Additional Language as these are not areas in which either of us has particular expertise. The materials produced by the NLS seem generally helpful, but our impression is that the practice recommended is generally just good practice which should benefit all children, such as multi-sensory teaching and the use of props and prompts to focus attention and encourage talk.

Boys

The same goes for boys. Our early start to formal education disadvantages boys (see pages 80-81), and many need extra help to make progress. Boys seem to benefit from a more structured teaching environment, plenty of variety and interactivity, an element of competition (e.g. games, team points), short bursts of skills teaching with immediate feedback on their performance, and opportunities to read and write about things that interest them. Catering for boys is again a case of good teaching - finding suitable resources, ensuring you give them motivating tasks, and adjusting teaching style to suit their needs.

Pupil attainment tracking

However, recognition that teaching is about meeting the needs of individuals does not mean we are over-impressed by the latest political craze for Pupil Attainment Tracking (PAT), i.e. adjusting teaching to reflect children's progress on specific elements in standardised tests. We wish politicians could understand that teaching is not an exact science and that attention to test results is a very, very small part of 'assessment for learning'. In real life this involves a plethora of professional knowledge and understanding, including:

- knowledge about the psychology of each child in the class and of children in general;
- knowledge about each pupil's personality, background and interests;
- adjusting practice day-to-day, on the basis of observation and, often, intuition (Did Alex have breakfast this morning? Is Emma's behaviour due to the high wind outside? Does Sam's tearstained face indicate the death of a hamster or something more profound?).

If PAT is given undue prominence, and turns into another pointless exercise in bureaucracy, not only will it fail to deliver results, but it will become counter-productive, distracting teachers once again from getting on with the job.

Inclusion and behavioural problems

Recognition of the needs of the individual pupil is at the heart of our inclusion policy, and the NLS has always emphasised the importance of inclusion in the Literacy Hour. Given sensitive teaching and adequate support in terms of additional adults, this inclusive policy is generally successful and welcomed by teachers. However inclusion does not always work in the case of children with behavioural difficulties. Unless their behaviour can be contained (and this involves specialist training for teachers and TAs, and constant effective support), they can disrupt the education of the whole class. Our children can't afford to have their literacy education spoilt in this way – and we can't expect teachers to strive over and above the course of duty to contain one child at the expense of the many. For this reason, we believe that more provision should be made for the separate education of emotionally and behaviourally disturbed children.

Maintaining a Balance

In 1990, Sue organised a campaign for *Balance in the teaching of language and literacy skills*. It was the era of 'real books'; phonics and grammar were considered the work of the devil; direct teaching was completely out of fashion, and teachers were required merely to 'facilitate children's learning'. The *Balance Manifesto* voiced the modest proposal that the profession should strike a balance between teaching and learning; between context-based literacy and attention to the way language works, and between 'real' books and structured teaching materials. However, such was the paranoia of the time that people did not dare question the accepted orthodoxy. One deputy head said, *I agree with everything you say, but it's more than my job's worth to say so publicly*.

In just over a decade, the educational pendulum in many schools swung to the opposite extreme. Rigid application to the Literacy Hour, the use of text extracts, language worksheets and never a 'real book' in sight, endless direct teaching while children sit, silent and glassy-eyed, in the 'literacy corner' and everything planned (on paper, in boxes) to the lowest common denominator of tedium. This was not what the National Literacy Strategy intended, but it's what you get when schools are subjected to a punitive Ofsted regime, a high-stakes tests-and-targets ethos, and endless pressure from LEAs themselves under pressure from central government.

The English education system sometimes seems to us like a complex system of Chinese whispers, each whisperer along the line helping to turn simple principles into terrible dreary orthodoxies. When the NLS came in one head teacher – clearly at the end of a whispering chain – said: *I fear we're sentencing our children to seven years hard labour – with no possibility of remission*.

What we can't understand is why committed knowledgeable professionals are prepared to accept what they know is claptrap. Why did we let the real books movement get so out of hand? Why would anyone accept 'seven years hard labour' on behalf of their children? Over the last twenty-five years we have seen a culture of orthodoxy within the teaching profession (at least in England – our impression is that it is less so in Wales, Scotland and Northern Ireland) which has been seriously damaging to the children whose interests we are all, at heart, desperate to serve.

Perhaps it's wishful thinking, but we detect that this culture is starting to break down. We are beginning to meet teachers who are prepared to say: *I think this is wrong and I'm not going to do it*. The mood is summed up in the story of a young teacher who stood up to her head teacher, local authority advisers and Ofsted, and refused to introduce formal literacy work in the first term of reception. (Goodness knows why they were asking her to do it – probably because they themselves were under pressure from somewhere and had misread the Chinese whispers). We hope we're right, and teachers will continue to resist the dead hand of orthodoxy, and to stand up for a balanced approach to the education of the children in their care.

Children need creativity, and they also need basic skills. The teaching of skills need not – should not – be boring; indeed, the creativity of teaching is seeking out the fun to be had in every lesson. Balance is common sense, and most of the teachers we've met have that in bucketloads. If they apply it to the whispers they hear, perhaps the National Primary Strategy will at last be successful and **all** our children will (a) learn to read and write and (b) have a good time doing so.

Appendix 1: Drama Activities

Role-play

In the Early Years, this is children's 'pretend play' in the role-play corner. Later, pupils can work in pairs or groups to take on the personae of characters in the subject under discussion. Different groups can role-play different scenes, to be put 'under the spotlight' for the rest to watch. Or the whole class could be involved in a 'public meeting' to discuss issues like *Should the High Street be closed to traffic?*.

Teacher in role

The teacher takes on a suitable role within the drama, to direct operations and develop children's understanding. It helps to have a prop (e.g. a cloak or clipboard) which indicates when you are in role, so that you can revert to 'teacher' when necessary.

Hot-seating

A pupil takes on the role of a character from fiction, history or any area of the curriculum, and the rest of the group question him/her about his involvement, opinions, feelings, etc.

Freeze-frame

Groups of children create 'living tableaux' of significant moments from a story or from what they know of a topic. Individuals can be asked to describe and comment on their role in a tableau.

Forum theatre

The class observes while one group acts out a scene. The audience can stop the drama at any point and suggest how characters should proceed in order to solve the problem or issue being explored.

Physical theatre

Great for teaching scientific processes. Pupils become, e.g., blood corpuscles, molecules, planets, animals in a food chain, and work out how to illustrate the process through movement and mime.

Role on the wall

The teacher draws an outline of a person on the board. Using evidence from their reading or knowledge of the character, pupils provide words describing how the character looks (to be written outside the outline) and his/her personality, feelings and opinions (written inside the outline).

Thought-tracking

One pupil acts the part of a character, providing the spoken words. Another provides a running commentary on his/her inner thoughts.

Readers' theatre

As a group or class, pupils prepare a reading of a text – which could be their own composition – experimenting with effects of voices (e.g. individual, choral, echoes), sound effects and musical accompaniment. This is then presented to an audience or recorded on tape for presentation.

Polished performance

Pupils rehearse and learn a play – published script or their own work – for performance to an audience, possibly using costumes, props and lighting to enhance the performance.

Literacy: what works? © Sue Palmer and Pie Corbett, Nelson Thornes, 2003

Appendix 2: Talking Sentences and Stories

Mr Copycat
The teacher says a sentence and the children repeat it – this can be escalated to include two, three or more sentences. Vary this by speaking slowly, quickly, musically, loudly, quietly. Use simple, compound and complex sentences. Practise the sorts of sentences that you will need in your writing.

Echo stories
The teacher says each sentence of a story or passage and the children chant them after her.

Follow the thread
Start the story off. Pause every so often so that the children can make up the next sentence. It can help to start the sentence, e.g. *At that moment...*

Hot seating
Interview characters from a story – what are their ambitions, fears, expectations?

Story play
Provide the basic props for children to use in their play, e.g. felt people, dolls, animals, dressing up clothes, characters on a magnetic board, magical objects.

Maps and pictures
Use story picture maps to invent stories or pictures to prompt places, characters and events.

Role-play area
Convert the role-play area into a story scene – three bears cave, fairy castle, forest; Asgard, Olympus, a Roman forum.

Using questions
Make the classroom a place where 'making up' stories is a simple everyday activity. Use questions to create simple problem/resolution tales or take a well-loved text and adapt it.

Learn and tell
To help **you** learn a story, put it on tape and play it in the car every morning! Once the children know a story, get them retelling in pairs and circles.

Story circle
Pass a story round a small circle, adding a sentence each.

Act it out
This really helps children internalise the basic structure and patterns in a narrative. The teacher takes the class in to the hall and tells the story. Everyone acts the tale out.

The storyteller's hat/chair.
Whenever you tell a story, put on your special 'storyteller's hat' or 'coat'. Children who have a story to tell are allowed to don it as well. In the same vein, having a special decorated chair for telling stories can also act as a spur to storytelling.

Puppets and masks
Make story character puppets or masks to use when telling tales – farmer, princess, wolf; Theseus, Ariadne, Minotaur and so on.

Appendix 3: Promoting Reading

1. Read to them
In the earliest stages, read picture books – five or six times a day. These need not take ages – but it is important. As well as enthusing them to read for themselves, it provides models of written language, without which children will find it difficult to write their own stories. Encourage children to increasingly join in with well-loved stories, until they have memorised the whole tale.

2. Keep on reading to them!
As children learn to listen and enjoy your reading, start to read without showing the pictures. This encourages them to make the pictures in their own heads. Children reared in a television age have to learn this art. Go on reading to them throughout the primary years. Not only will they learn to create their own images, they will absorb through exposure and repetition the language patterns of successful writing.

3. The right books
In the book corner check that you have a wide variety of texts: comics, annuals, jokebooks, poetry, TV tie-ins, stories and information books about things that interest children. Provide 'quick-reads' for strugglers.

4. Poetry journals
Every week stick a new nursery rhyme or poem in a journal to be learned at home. Over a primary career that would make over 200 poems! As well as the sheer pleasure of having a repertoire of poems in their heads, this will train children's auditory memory – important for learning in general, but especially for literacy.

5. Grabbers
Make sure you have 'cool' books to read – including 'boy appeal' – from Michael Lawrence's *Toilet of Doom* to Paul Jennings, Anthony Horowitz and Morris Gleitzman.

6. Series
Provide series of books – once hooked into the series, *Dilly The Dinosaur* provides practice at one level, plus the child internalises the author's style and themes.

7. Dodgy sevens
Hold a meeting with Y3 parents to ensure that they continue to work on reading at home. If they can, it really helps to keep up the bedtime reading at this stage. If they can't, suggest they get a tape recorder (see 13 below).

8. Book clubs and sessions for parents
Circulate books with book swaps. Run book clubs. Hold book evenings for parents.

9. Slippers
Run lunchtime 'buddy' reading clubs for those who do not get support at home.

10. Computer-based material
Use computer games and information sites as a way to motivate reading practice. Use good reading/writing sites such as Poetryzone at **www.poetryzone.ndirect.co.uk**; at **www.youngwriter.org** you will find the Young Writer website.

11. Fuss and ado
Celebrate reading in assemblies, create 'poet-trees', tape stories, make poetry programmes, perform stories and poems for others. Hold weekly 'recommendation' sessions – where children take turns to introduce a book, and read a short extract to tantalise the class. Develop a buzz about books.

12. Homework
Use homework to ensure regular reading, e.g. poems to prepare for the next lesson, short stories to read and be ready to discuss, information leaflets to extract points to debate.

13. Tapes versus TV
Parents nowadays are under tremendous pressure to let children have a television in their bedroom. Help them resist by promoting audiotapes instead of TV. Set up an audiotape library in school and encourage pupils to listen rather than watch.

14. Authors in school
Invite authors, drama groups, storytellers and artists into school as a regular feature (through Speaking of Books – see Appendix 5). Make theatre visits. Take magazines *Books for Keeps* (6 Brightfield Rd, Lee, London SE12 8QF), and *Young Writer* (Glebe House, Weobley, Hereford, HR4 8SD).

Beware of 'Death by Extract'.

Of course, extracts are handy. If you are investigating different strategies for writing an engaging opening to a story, it is helpful to look at how a number of authors tackle this. However, to develop a love of reading, for reading to become a powerful experience and for genuine appreciation to take place, then whole texts have to be read. Comprehension based on extracts will only ever be partial. Key Stage 2 classes should always have a novel on the go. Would you really want children to leave your school never having met *The Iron Man, The Hodgeheg, Charlotte's Web, The Battle of Bubble and Squeak, The Eighteenth Emergency, Stig of the Dump, Why the Whales Came, Tom's Midnight Garden, Carrie's War, Fireweed, The Machine Gunners, Skellig, Holes, The Hobbit*...?

Teach in units

Most schools now have moved beyond teaching isolated bits of literacy into working in larger units. Narrative blocks lend themselves to the building up of resources schools need for bringing reading alive. For instance – Year 4 Term 3 might become an Anne Fine term. Into the garage box goes a half-class set of *Bill's New Frock*. Other Fine books can be bunched into sets of five for guided reading; videos of interviews with the author, televised versions, downloaded material from websites, biographies brought out. A national scheme might provide an author website so that schools can tap into video material of authors discussing how they write, where ideas come from, providing advice for young writers. Poets could read and discuss their poems onto CD-ROMs for schools to use.

Library services

School Library Services need to be strengthened to keep schools abreast of new books, to help develop school and class libraries, to co-ordinate author visits, to provide book boxes and packs. Teachers cannot be expected to read everything that comes out – library services have to be rebuilt to help us place reading back in the centre of education. LEAs should all have regular secondments for storytellers, poets and authors to work with teachers and schools. We have music teachers who visit schools – why not regular storytellers?

Literacy: what works? © Sue Palmer and Pie Corbett, Nelson Thornes, 2003

Appendix 4: NLS Publications (at summer 2003)

Downloadable from www.standards.dfes.gov.uk/literacy/publications. Those in print are available in paper form from 0845 6022260.

Framework for teaching
The National Literacy Strategy – Framework for teaching YR to Y6
The National Literacy Strategy – Framework for teaching: Additional guidance
The National Literacy Strategy – Glossary of terms
Guidance on the organisation of the National Literacy Strategy in Reception classes
Target setting at Key Stage 2
ICT in the Literacy Hour: Whole class teaching
ICT in the Literacy Hour: Independent work and guided reading

Word level
Phonics – Progression in Phonics for whole class teaching (includes video)
Phonics – Progression in Phonics for whole class teaching CD-ROM
Spelling bank: Lists of words and activities for the KS2 spelling objectives

Sentence level
Grammar for Writing (Key Stage 2)
Grammar for Writing leaflets

Text level
Illustrative target statements for reading
Every lesson counts
Target statements for writing
Developing Early Writing
Marking Guidelines for Writing
Quality text to support the teaching of writing
Shared Writing on School Placement (KS1 and KS2)
Teaching writing: Support material for text level objectives (fliers)
Literacy Across the Curriculum: strand tracker

Inclusion
Towards the National Curriculum for English
Including all children in the literacy hour and daily mathematics lesson
Supporting the target setting process: Guidance for effective target setting for pupils with SEN
Supporting pupils with SEN in the Literacy Hour
NLNS – Guidance on Teaching Able Children
Supporting pupils learning English as an Additional Language: revised edition

Planning
An example of NLS medium-term planning
Year 6 – Planning Exemplification 2002–2003
Year 6 – Planning Exemplification 2001–2002
Year 4 Term 1 Planning Exemplification: Plays
Year 4 and 5 Planning Exemplification
Year 3 Term 1 Planning Exemplification: Report

Targeted support

Easter schools guidance
Helping children achieve throughout Year 6 - English and Mathematics
2001 Revision Guidance for Year 6 Pupils
1999 Revision Guidance for Year 6 Pupils (includes Activity Resources Sheets)
1999 Revision Guidance for Year 6 Pupils – Suggested Lesson Plans
Year 6 Refresher Pack

Intervention programmes

Year 6 Literacy Booster Lessons: 2003
NLNS Intervention programmes
Further Literacy Support: Resource Pack
*Additional Literacy Support (ALS) (*includes video*)*
Early Literacy Support – Top-up sessions
Early Literacy Support Programme: session materials for teaching assistants
Year 5 Booster Units
Year 6 Booster Units
Guidance on Organising Literacy and Numeracy Booster Classes
Early Literacy Support Programme: materials for teachers working in partnership with teaching assistants
Early Literacy Support: fliers

Transition KS2 – KS3

Year 7 Sentence Level Bank
Year 7 Speaking and Listening Bank
Year 7 Spelling Bank
Framework for teaching English: Years 7, 8 and 9
Transition from Year 6 to Year 7 English: Units of work
Making Links 2002: guidance for summer schools and Year 7 support programmes
Auditing and reviewing a subject in Key Stages 2 and 3 in middle schools

Research and evaluation

Progress in International Reading Literacy Study: Reading all over the world
Watching and Learning 3
Watching and Learning: Evaluation of the Implementation of the NLNS: First Annual Report and Summary
Implementation of the NLS: Final Report
Implementation of the NLS: A summary for primary schools
National Literacy Strategy: Review of research and other related evidence
Evaluation of National Literacy Project: Summary report
Watching and Learning 2

Miscellaneous

The Primary Leadership Programme: information for participating schools
Raising standards in middle schools
Building on improvement
Literacy Co-ordinators' Handbook
Working with teaching assistants – a good practice guide
National Literacy Strategy – Cohort 2 intensive training materials
Activity Resource Bank Booklets
*The National Literacy Strategy Training Pack (*includes videos and audio cassettes*)*

National Primary Strategy 2003
Excellence and Enjoyment

Related QCA publications
Downloadable from www.qca.org.uk/publications or in paper form from 01787 884444

A Language in common: Assessing English as an additional language
Curriculum guidance for the foundation stage
Planning, Teaching and Assessing the Curriculum for Pupils with Learning Difficulties
Target setting and assessment in the National Literacy Strategy
Teaching Speaking and Listening in Key Stages 1 and 2
Standards at Key Stage 2 English and Mathematics
Standards at Key Stage 1 English and Mathematics
Working with gifted and talented children: KS1 and 2 English and Mathematics
Implications for teaching and learning from the 2002 tests KS1 English
Implications for teaching and learning from the 2002 tests KS2 English

Related OFSTED publications
Downloadable from www.ofsted.gov.uk or in paper form from 0870 6005522

Strategies in action
The National Literacy Strategy: An Interim Evaluation
An Evaluation of the first year of the National Literacy Strategy
The NLS: The second year
The NLS in Special Schools: 1998-2000
The NLS: The first four years 1998-2002
Teaching of Literacy and Mathematics in Reception Classes: A survey by HMI
The Curriculum in Successful Primary Schools

Appendix 5: Recommended Resources

Resource	Author	Publisher
Highlighting tape and many other teaching aids		TTS (0800 318686)
The Phonics Handbook ('Jolly Phonics')	Sue Lloyd	Jolly Learning Co
Penpals (handwriting scheme)		Cambridge University Press
Nelson Handwriting (New Edition)	Anita Warwick and John Jackman	Nelson Thornes
Searchlights for Spelling	Pie Corbett	Cambridge University Press
Big Book Spelling	Sue Palmer and Michaela Morgan	Ginn and Co
Wordshark (spelling CD-ROM)		White Space Ltd (0208 748 5927)
How to Detect and Manage Dyslexia	Philomena Ott	Heinemann
Dyslexia: Literacy Strategies for the Classroom		Croydon SEN Support Service (0208 656 6551)
Grammar Success	Pie Corbett	Oxford University Press
Big Book Grammar	Sue Palmer and Michaela Morgan	Heinemann
Skeleton Poster Books for Grammar (and OHTs)	Sue Palmer	TTS (0800 318686)
Exploring the writing of genres	Beverley Derewianka	UKRA (01763 241188)
Skeleton Poster Books (and OHTs) for text types	Sue Palmer	TTS (0800 318686)
Thinking Skills and Eye Q	Oliver Caviglioli, Ian Harris and Bill Tindall	Network Educational Press (01785 225515)
How to Teach Writing Across the Curriculum at Key Stage 1		
How to Teach Writing Across the Curriculum at Key Stage 2	Sue Palmer	David Fulton Publishers
How to Teach Story Writing at Key Stage 1		
How to Teach Fiction Writing at Key Stage 2	Pie Corbett	David Fulton Publishers
Jumpstart! Literacy games	Pie Corbett	David Fulton Publishers
Connections (cross-curricular literacy resources)	Ed. Sue Palmer	Oxford University Press
Catapults and Kingfishers – teaching poetry	Pie Corbett and Brian Moses	Oxford University Press
The Poetry Book	Ed. Anthony Wilson & Sian Hughes	The Poetry Society, 22 Betterton St, WC2H 9BU
Poetry in the making	Ted Hughes	Faber
100+ Ideas for Drama	Anna Scher and Charles Verrall	Heinemann Ed. Books
Poetic Writing in the Primary School	Pie Corbett	Kent Reading & Language Development Centre, Christchurch College, Canterbury.
Write your own Chillers	Pie Corbett	Belitha Books at www.chrysalisbooks.co.uk
Write your own Thrillers		Belitha Books at www.chrysalisbooks.co.uk
Start Talking (R-Y3)	Pie Corbett and Ruth Thomson	LDA
The address book of children's authors and illustrators	Ed. Gervase Phinn	
Creating Writers	James Carter	Routledge Falmer
The Reading Environment	Aidan Chambers	Thimble Press
Tell Me: Children Reading and Talk	Aidan Chambers	Thimble Press
The Meaning Makers	Gordon Wells	Hodder and Stoughton Educational Books
The Works 2	Ed. Pie Corbett and Brian Moses	Macmillan Children's Books
Poems for Year 3, 4, 5 and 6	Ed. Pie Corbett	Macmillan Children's Books
The King's Pyjamas	Ed. Pie Corbett	Belitha Books at www.chrysalisbooks.co.uk

Snow White in New York	Fiona French	Oxford University Press
Badger's Parting Gifts	Susan Varley	HarperCollins
The Castle of Adventure	Enid Blyton	Macmillan Children's Books
The Northern Lights	Philip Pullman	Scholastic
Flat Stanley	Jeff Brown	Mammoth
The Toilet of Doom	Michael Lawrence	Orchard Books
Dilly the Dinosaur series	Tony Bradman	Mammoth

Paul Jennings published by Puffin
Anthony Horowitz published by Walker Books
Morris Gleitzman published by Puffin and Macmillan Children's Books

The Iron Man	Ted Hughes	Faber
The Machine Gunners	Robert Westall	Macmillan Children's Books
Skellig	David Almond	Hodder Children's Books
Holes	Louis Sachar	Bloomsbury Children's Books
The Hobbit	J.R.R. Tolkein	HarperCollins
Bill's New Frock	Ann Fine	Egmont Books
Why the Whales Came	Michael Morpurgo	Egmont Books
The Hodgeheg	Dick King Smith	
Charlotte's Web	E.B.White	
The Battle of Bubble and Squeak	Philippa Pearce	
The 18th Emergency	Betsy Byars	
Stig of the Dump	Clive King	
Tom's Midnight Garden	Philippa Pearce	
Carrie's War	Nina Bawden	
Fireweed	Jill Paton Walsh	all published by Puffin
The Little Book of Role-Play (and other 'little books)	Sally Featherstone	Featherstone Education Ltd (0185 888 1212)
A Corner to Learn (role-play areas for KS1 and 2)	Neil Griffiths	Nelson Thornes
Speaking, Listening and Drama Y1-2,3-4, 5-6	John Airs and Chris Ball	Hopscotch Publishing (01926 744227)
Puppet Talk	Lillian Coppock	TTS (0800 318686)
The Music-Makers Approach	Hannah Mortimer	NASEN (01827 311500)
Music in Action with Big Books	Gaunt and Dunville	Lovely Music (01937 832946)
That's Science (science through song)	Tim Harding	Network Educational Press (01785 225515)
Picture This: guided imagery for circle time	Murray White (and many other circle time materials)	Lucky Duck Publishing (0117 973 2881)
History resources on tape (Egyptians, Romans, etc)		Sound Learning (01543 467787)
Maths Call (YR to Y6)	Peter Clarke	HarperCollins Publishers
Helping Young Children to Listen	Ros Bayley and Lynn Broadbent	Lawrence Educational Publications (01922 643833)
Time to Talk	Alison Schroeder	LDA (01223 357788)
Thinking Allowed (video and booklet)		Queens School, Richmond-on-Thames (0208 940 3580) 01704 501730
The English Speaking Board (assessments in spoken English)		
Thinking, Reading, Writing	Keith Topping	Continuum Press
Talk First: Voices in the Park	Chris Onono, Liz Miller and Joy Pickard	Stockton-on-Tees Education Service (01642 397372)
Speaking Frames (Years 3–6)	Sue Palmer	David Fulton Publishers
Smooth Transitions	Ros Bayley and Sally Featherstone	Featherstone Education Ltd (0185 888 1212)
Creative Storytelling	Jack Zipes	Routledge
Storytelling, the missing link in story writing by Teresa Grainger in *Connecting and Creating*	Ed. Sue Ellis and Colin Mills	UKRA (01763 241188)
Speaking of Books	Jan Powling	020 8692 4704

Literacy: what works? © Sue Palmer and Pie Corbett, Nelson Thornes, 2003